Teaching the Scientific Literature Review

Recent Titles in the
Libraries Unlimited Guided Inquiry Series

Seeking Meaning: A Process Approach to Library and Information Services, Second Edition
Carol C. Kuhlthau

Guided Inquiry: Learning in the 21st Century
Carol C. Kuhlthau, Leslie K. Maniotes, and Ann K. Caspari

Guided Inquiry Design: A Framework for Inquiry in Your School
Carol C. Kuhlthau, Leslie K. Maniotes, and Ann K. Caspari

A Guided Inquiry Approach to High School Research
Randell K. Schmidt

Teaching the Scientific Literature Review

Collaborative Lessons for Guided Inquiry

SECOND EDITION

Randell K. Schmidt, Maureen M. Smyth, and Virginia K. Kowalski

Libraries Unlimited Guided Inquiry

LIBRARIES UNLIMITED

AN IMPRINT OF ABC-CLIO, LLC
Santa Barbara, California • Denver, Colorado • Oxford, England

Library of Congress Cataloging-in-Publication Data

Schmidt, Randell K., author.
  [Lessons for a scientific literature review]
  Teaching the scientific literature review : collaborative lessons for guided inquiry / Randell K. Schmidt, Maureen M. Smyth, and Virginia K. Kowalski. — Second edition.
      pages cm
  Revision of: Lessons for a scientific literature review. 2008.
  Includes bibliographical references and index.
    ISBN 978-1-61069-739-2 (paperback : acid-free paper) — ISBN 978-1-61069-740-8 (ebook)
  1. Scientific literature—Study and teaching (Secondary)   2. Technical writing—Study and teaching (Secondary)   3. Research—Study and teaching (Secondary)   4. Peer review—Study and teaching (Secondary)   5. Science publishing—Study and teaching (Secondary)   6. Science—Study and teaching (Secondary)—Activity programs.   I. Smyth, Maureen M., author.   II. Kowalski, Virginia K., author.   III. Title.
    Q225.5.S347   2014
    507.1'2—dc23   2013050951

ISBN: 978-1-61069-739-2
EISBN: 978-1-61069-740-8

18 17 16 15 14   1 2 3 4 5

This book is also available on the World Wide Web as an eBook.
Visit www.abc-clio.com for details.

Libraries Unlimited
An Imprint of ABC-CLIO, LLC

ABC-CLIO, LLC
130 Cremona Drive, P.O. Box 1911
Santa Barbara, California 93116-1911

This book is printed on acid-free paper ∞

Manufactured in the United States of America

This book is dedicated to all those 11th grade students
who actively participated in the SLR at Gill St. Bernard's
School and whose hard work, mature handling,
and interpretation of the material encouraged us to write
this book.

And to Peter, Doug, and Jim.

Contents

Foreword

An important challenge for high school educators is to prepare their college-bound students for success in undergraduate work. Students making the transition to college frequently find academic research especially difficult to master. This is particularly true when they are assigned to write a scientific literature review that forms the basis of academic research. Even students that have experience with research papers, extended essays, and capstone projects in high school are often confused and overwhelmed when confronted with this task. This book is a program for introducing students to the scientific literature review that leads to independence and academic success, essential for every student planning to engage in university study.

Teaching the Scientific Literature Review: Collaborative Lessons for Guided Inquiry is a valuable addition to the Guided Inquiry series that is based in my research on students' process of learning from a variety of sources described in the Information Search Process (ISP) (*Seeking Meaning*, Kuhlthau, 2004). The ISP describes seven stages in students' thoughts, feelings, and actions in the process of learning through inquiry. The ISP is an influential model in library and information science and widely applied in school and academic libraries. The foundational text in the series is *Guided Inquiry: Learning in the 21st Century* (Kuhlthau, Maniotes, and Caspari, 2007).

For more than a decade, Randell Schmidt and her colleagues have developed a systematic program of Guided Inquiry that has successfully and consistently led their students to research independence and academic success. They have shown the powerful impact inquiry learning has on the entire school that is a working lab for our research at CISSL, the Center for International Scholarship in School Libraries at Rutgers University. Randi and her coauthors share their exceptional expertise in this book.

Teaching the Scientific Literature Review: Collaborative Lessons for Guided Inquiry is a practical guide for teachers and librarians to teach students the steps of developing a scientific literature review that is aligned with the stages of the ISP and the Common Core State Standards (CCSS). It shows how to guide students toward independence in academic research and college readiness. The book makes a daunting task not only manageable, but also engaging and personally rewarding through tested lessons that provide guidance at each stage in the ISP. The authors offer lots of insider advice, including how to develop a hook that becomes the focus for the review. Assessment rubrics are incorporated for each stage of the ISP. The voices of students are heard throughout in descriptive quotes of their experience in the research process and examples of success. The high school students that have gone through the program found that they were well prepared to make the transition to college research and report that this was a critical part of their high school education that prepared them for college work.

This addition to the Guided Inquiry series is a companion to another book in the series (*A Guided Inquiry Approach to High School Research*, Schmidt, 2013). The purpose of these books is to prepare students for academic research and college readiness. They provide a program for developing high school students into independent academic scholars. Taken together, as companion texts, they offer a program for preparing students for successful academic research.

Carol Collier Kuhlthau, Professor Emerita
Rutgers, The State University of New Jersey

Preface

In the years between the publication of the first edition of *Lessons for a Scientific Literature Review: Guiding the Inquiry* and the publication of this second edition, there has been, some might argue, a seismic shift in the educational landscape. In 2010, the Common Core Learning Standards (CCSS) were released by the National Governors Association and the Council of Chief State School Officers. The CCSS were designed to align curricula and develop mastery for college as well as career ready skills in math and literacy. At the heart of the CCSS are necessary research skills. Such skills place inquiry in the center of current pedagogical discourse.

The word **inquiry** has attained a certain cache in education circles. Prior to the implementation of the Common Core, *inquiry* was often suggested as a panacea to move the focus of instruction from teacher centered to student centered. Unfortunately, the word had nebulous meaning to most teachers and administrators, even as they sought to develop inquiry-based lessons and schools purported to ascribe to inquiry-based instructional modes. *Teaching the Scientific Literature Review: Collaborative Lessons for Guided Inquiry* seeks to define inquiry and suggest a model for instruction that puts the student at the center of the learning; this is exactly what the Common Core is seeking to do, as well. In order for students to achieve mastery of Common Core performance skills, they must first know how to conduct research and present their findings in written and spoken form.

Inquiry has become an important buzz word, as it is now appropriately attached to fluency in research and media. Through an emphasis on research and textual analysis, the CCSS have made projects, such as the one outlined in the following pages of this book, timely and necessary. Schools need to create and implement research and inquiry projects to address the skills to meet the CCSS. Forty-five of 50 states are currently implementing the Common Core Curriculum, and many states are following Kentucky and New York's lead and implementing Common Core–aligned standardized assessments as well. Under consideration in New York is a proposal to add a research component to its High School ELA exam. By 2015, there will be, more than likely, cross-state assessments through the Partnership for Assessment of Readiness for College and Careers (PARCC) and the Smarter Balanced Assessment Consortium (SBAC).

Another important addition for many states is the development of the Next Generation Science Standards (NGSS). At the heart of these new standards is a clear expectation that students will conduct scientific investigation through a process of inquiry. As states move toward developing collaborative assessments and a Common Core- and/or NGSS-aligned curricula, it will be increasingly necessary for curricula to be clearly aligned with Common Core performance standards.

As the publication of the first edition of this book attested, strong research curricula existed before the Common Core. However, it is important that curricula, such as the project outlined in this book, clearly delineate the Common Core–aligned skills that students will develop through the Guided Inquiry process. Teachers and schools need curriculum materials that they can look to for guidance as they move forward to create Common Core–aligned lessons and assessment. This revised and updated edition of *Teaching the Scientific Literature Review: Collaborative Lessons for Guided Inquiry* will provide educators with the components necessary to successfully teach their students how to research and write a scientific literature review.

Acknowledgments

When a book is revised and updated, the person responsible for the revision must acknowledge the continued intellectual contributions of those original authors as well as newfound voices who add to and deepen the work.

Thus, I must first thank my original coauthors Maureen Smyth and Virginia Kowalski. They have made a meaningful and lasting contribution to the field of guided education with the original text which has been altered, amended, and embellished, as we have learned more from teaching the scientific literature review (SLR) since the original publication.

Contributions and insights of education from Sweden, Australia, Germany, and South Korea are acknowledged as educators around the world refer to and use the book to enhance their own curricula. Special thanks go to Goran Brolund, Marina Roslund, and Lena Fogelberg Carlsson of Sweden and to Lee Fitzgerald of Australia who have been with me teaching and improving aspects of the SLR for the last five years. Professor Ross Todd of Rutgers University and the Center for International Scholarship in School Libraries (CISSL) have become a constant resource for our program.

The revised book could not have been accomplished without the help of several fellow teachers and librarians. Special thanks go to historian Dr. John Ripton for his content critique and to my sons Joseph and Geoffrey Schmidt, veterans of urban public education, who provided invaluable assistance explaining and aligning the SLR curriculum with the Common Core Standards in the preface and in the workshops. Assistant Librarian Emilia Giordano provided extraordinary organizational assistance and contemporary media expertise with the revisions and the new content of the workshop plans. Hers was not an easy task and I am particularly grateful for her work. Editorial wonder woman Cecilia Rhodes helped to shepherd the corrections and production of the manuscript. Courtney Puglisi produced the Workshop Timeline and cheerfully assisted in producing the manuscript. Special thanks to students John Carlson Brown who provided samples from his works-cited pages of his research on antiepileptic drugs and Hannah Geldzahler who provided a sample of her analysis table. My thanks to librarian Claudia Hesler who kept me on target with digital resources, and to sister librarian Cynthia Washburn who lent her superior editorial skills as well as content expertise. Another reader, Dana Karnell Logoutte, provided insight and clarity to the content. No part of this edition could have been completed without all these determined former students and educators.

My heartfelt thanks go to editor Sharon Coatney who is a champion of progressive guided education and who truly knows her stuff! I am forever indebted to my mentor, Dr. Carol C. Kuhlthau, who wrote the foreword to the revision of the book and who must be acknowledged by all of us for leading the way to a more purposeful future for students and teachers engaged in guided inquiry.

Randell K. Schmidt

Part I

Teacher's Practicum

1

The Value of Inquiry-Based Research Projects

The primary role of the school in the 21st century will be determined, in large part, by a broader understanding of how students interact with information, and then structuring education to enable more interaction. For too long, at the high school and early college level, each academic discipline has been its own subject field—the history teacher knew all about U.S. History, the math teacher knew all about Algebra, and the biology teacher could teach all about Biology. Teachers were considered the experts, the authorities, while students learned only what the authorities taught. Knowledge was transferred from one head to the other—from an expert teacher to a rote-learning student. Understanding was an infrequent by-product.

The world of information has become a wilderness. Teachers who themselves explore the information wilderness can no longer claim complete mastery and certainly cannot "teach" a whole field of knowledge, but must focus on principles, models, and examples of that field. Today's environment is a world of endless, underorganized information. No single teacher, course, or textbook can possibly be an ultimate authority. Authority, while it has not disappeared, has dispersed, and knowledge, while it has increased, has not been concentrated. Thus, authority and knowledge are hiding in the wilderness of information. The student, on the other hand, still must be "taught" some content and must learn at least something about the subject at hand.

To resolve the contradiction of "unteachable" whole subjects and students seeking knowledge, teachers and students are forced to pick and choose what to teach and what to learn. One way to pick and choose what to teach and learn is to allow students a choice of subjects in guided inquiry-based projects. Here, the teacher, in the process of teaching, transforms from master to guide, and the student, in the process of inquiry, transforms from novice to master. In effect, guided inquiry through the wilderness of information changes the entire process of education as the student, teacher, and librarian become fellow travelers into the unknown wilderness and emerge from the Information Search Process (ISP; Kuhlthau, 2004) and the inquiry itself as discoverers of a new world of knowledge (Kuhlthau & Todd, 2007b). To fulfill the role of information experts, librarians must collaborate with principals, teachers, students, and even with the information itself. Teaching the Scientific Literature Review (SLR) is precisely such a productive collaboration.

The essential contradiction in the collaboration between science teachers and librarians is in the sharing of limited instruction time and teaching opportunities. A science teacher considering a research assignment, such as the SLR, must sacrifice content time to the librarian who guides a student through a research inquiry. Thus, process encroaches upon content, or so it seems. In reality, this collaboration (CISSL, 2007) will provide evidence to all that the process enlivens and enhances student interaction with scientific content, and results in more understanding, deeper knowledge, and greater enthusiasm as the student encounters authentic scientific reporting from the real world and learns how to manage it.

In addition to acknowledging the contradiction between teaching content and process, the authors also acknowledge the seeming differences between the science teacher's understanding of scientific inquiry in the classroom and the librarian's understanding of guided inquiry during the research process.

As adopted by the National Science Teachers Association in October 2004, its understanding of scientific inquiry is as stated below:

> The *National Science Education Standards* defines scientific inquiry as "the diverse ways in which scientists study the natural world and propose explanations based on the evidence derived from their work. Scientific inquiry also refers to the activities through which students develop knowledge and understanding of scientific ideas, as well as an understanding of how scientists study the natural world." The Science as Inquiry Standard in NSES includes the abilities necessary to do scientific inquiry and understanding about scientific inquiry.
>
> Scientific inquiry reflects how scientists come to understand the natural world, and it is at the heart of how students learn. From a very early age, children interact with their environment, ask questions, and seek ways to answer those questions. Understanding science content is significantly enhanced when ideas are anchored to inquiry experiences.
>
> Scientific inquiry is a powerful way of understanding science content. Students learn how to ask questions and use evidence to answer them. In the process of learning the strategies of scientific inquiry, students learn to conduct an investigation and collect evidence from a variety of sources, develop an explanation from the data, and communicate and defend their conclusion.
>
> The National Science Teachers Association (NSTA) recommends that all K–16 teachers embrace scientific inquiry and is committed to helping educators make it the centerpiece of the science classroom. The use of scientific inquiry will help ensure that students develop a deep understanding of science and scientific inquiry. (NSTA, 2007. Used with permission.)

Meanwhile, the librarian's understanding of inquiry can be found on the website for the Center for International Scholarship in School Libraries (CISSL) at Rutgers University, which sets out the definition for guided inquiry as:

> Guided Inquiry is carefully planned, closely supervised targeted intervention of an instructional team of librarians and teachers to guide students

through curriculum based inquiry units that build deep knowledge and deep understanding of a curriculum topic, and gradually lead towards independent learning. Guided Inquiry is grounded in a constructivist approach to learning, based on the Information Search Process developed by Kuhlthau, for developing students' competence with learning from a variety of sources while enhancing their understanding of the content areas of the curriculum. (Kuhlthau & Todd, 2007a)

Guided Inquiry as an approach to learning does not conflict with standards-based education. Standards define what is to be learned in each subject, and inquiry defines how learning might be enabled. Through inquiry learning, students are able to transform a myriad of information inputs made available through information sources to personal knowledge. . . . Guided Inquiry is an approach that focuses on the process of thinking that builds understandings *by engaging students in stimulating encounters with information—encounters which capture their interest and attention, and which motivate and direct their ongoing inquiry* [italics added]. Students learn by constructing their own understandings of these experiences by building on what they already know to form a personal perspective of the world. Underpinning the inquiry process is a thinking process that requires extensive interrogation and exploration of ideas and formulation of thoughts before moving on to collecting, organizing, and presenting ideas in ways which demonstrate personal understanding and ownership. The school library plays an active and integral role in developing meaningful inquiry in curriculum by enabling students to address these essential questions through resource-based learning tasks. (Kuhlthau & Todd, 2007c)

National standards have been incorporated into the SLR workshops. The standards outline desired student-learning outcomes as well as a vision for educational progress. The Common Core State Standards for English Language Arts & Literacy in History/Social Studies, Science and Technical Subjects cover competency levels for grades 11 and 12 (junior and senior year) of high school. Standards have been adopted by 45 states in the United States and are expected to indicate a desired level of educational preparation for high school graduation and future educational or vocational endeavors.

For all teachers and librarians using this Scientific Literature Review guided inquiry curriculum, I have included 11th and 12th grade level standards from:

- Writing Standards for Literacy in History/Social Sciences, Science, and Technical Subjects
- Writing Standards
- Reading Standards for Informational Text
- Reading Standards for Literacy in Science and Technical Subjects
- Speaking and Listening Standards

Teachers who are considering using the SLR as a cross-curricular project should especially consider the application of multiple standards in the project.

The authors also acknowledge Extended Essay standards being adopted internationally by Sweden and Australia as a means to ensure educational competencies before high school graduation for collegiate education or vocational training.

Although the Association of College and Research Libraries' *Information Literacy Competency Standards for Higher Education* (ACRL, 2000) are not included here, the standards, too, outline information-literacy competencies in the higher-education setting. By referencing these standards, we intend to highlight our specific learning outcome goals. In addition, as specific sets of standards are utilized by an instructor's school, instructor communication and documentation may be customized. However, we recognize that curriculum is locally governed and that the standards included in each workshop represent possible outcome achievements. As lessons are adapted and customized to suit the needs and preferences of individual instructors, standards, too, will need to be adjusted accordingly.

The authors of this guide to the SLR are librarians who for the last 14 years have collaborated with science teachers to co-teach the SLR to upper-grade level high school students. The book introduces a tested curriculum for guided inquiry to the SLR. As a student-centered project, the SLR curriculum embraces the NSES's definition of inquiry-based science learning and espouses CISSL's guided inquiry approach to a scientific research paper for students gathering and learning about new scientific information and knowledge.

The concepts of inquiry in scientific education and educational librarianship are grounded in the questions, the process of questioning and information gathering, and personal learning that a student experiences. For the science teacher, inquiry is the basis of learning about the scientific world, and for the librarian, inquiry is the basis of learning, period.

The Junior Year SLR has been taught annually since 1999 at Gill St. Bernard's School, an independent, college-preparatory school in New Jersey. The unit is a collaborative student inquiry–based learning project conducted and graded by the school's science teachers (chemistry, biology, physics, and psychology) and the librarian. The final result is a student-produced SLR. The student chooses a topic of personal interest linked to his science class subject(s). The librarian instructs the student in how to perform the necessary research (database refresher, searching for recent general press, peer-reviewed studies, etc.) and how to successfully synthesize and integrate the new information into a final product (i.e., how to write the required paper sections). The science teacher oversees and grades the content of the topic research.

Of course, one New Jersey independent school's curriculum for a SLR cannot be blindly inserted and applied to all schools. For suggestions in the replication of this project and a reminder of the need for flexibility in the curriculum's application, see Chapter 6: **Replication and Flexibility Squared**.

The kind of educational process we are engaging in with these collaborations postulates a dynamic sense of information that asserts that once encountered, information does not stagnate but interacts with existing, known information and causes a change in thinking. This change causes other thoughts, ideas, and concepts to change. Information is dynamic, and the dynamics of information deepen the search conducted and the knowledge gained. This collaboration of the science student with the new information can fulfill a personal information need. At times, it also fulfills an emotional need, and in most cases acts as a stimulant for new ways of thinking. As teachers and students alike know, "Research changes the mind." The following student illustrates that change:

> I didn't want to do the project on the effects of pesticides because I was afraid of what I thought I was going to learn. I grew up on a farm. My dad's side of the family are all farmers. I didn't want to face the fact that my father's cancer could have been induced by being raised on a farm that used pesticides. My dad died when I was eight of pancreatic cancer. I was very stubborn and reluctant but I finally decided (after not finding enough on pathological lying) to research pesticides.
>
> After reading the reports that show the correlation between pesticide exposure and breast and prostate cancer, it was very clear, in some of the studies, those children who lived in households of farmers using pesticides contained traces of those pesticides in their urine. The study sparked my interest in the environment—what we're putting into the soil. I saw a big change in myself to be motivated to do something. If pesticides exposure is what ultimately killed my father, how many others could it kill? (Brooke Donaldson, student, Gill St. Bernard's School, 2007)

While Brooke's reaction, based on reading only a few studies, was quite strong, her response provides evidence of her growing awareness of the possible risks of pesticide use.

Moving beyond the paradigm of strict content transfer, the collaboration between student, science teacher, librarian, and information is a road map to new territories of learning. The student chooses what to think about, and the teacher and librarian act as guides in that choice—not because the teacher and librarian know everything the student needs to know, but because they have entered the information wilderness more often, have undertaken the ISP, and understand how this model works.

This collaboration of guiding instructors and information-seeking student is an active partnership in the encounter with new information sources. The continuation of the partnership depends upon whether the student can make personal meaning of the new information. Therefore, the goal of finding the information depends upon the student-centered perspective. It is not about what the teacher or librarian wants, but rather they focus upon what the student can make of the information search. The collaboration depends upon the student's own interest and how that interest can be enriched and deepened.

Collaboration with information is analogous to collaboration between people. In fact, it is collaboration between people because, ultimately, people are the source of most information. When questions, ideas, information, and people all come together, it may be the most fruitful and human of collaborations. In the SLR project, inquiry is triggered by a question the student presents. The scientific inquiry is enhanced by the guided collaboration between the teachers, librarians, students, and information. These guided inquiry-based scientific projects (CISSL, 2007) allow for a more personal interaction with information and produce deeper knowledge, as well as more meaningful results.

The SLR project is a different type of science project than most students are accustomed to. Rather than incorporating physical elements and researching or examining by hands-on experimentation, the SLR is a minds-on experiment. The SLR creates the opportunity for a student to mentally play with a large amount of scientific information and toy with an idea or ideas that the information points or responds to.

In the context of Einstein's concept of the thought experiment (Ireson, 2005), the SLR affords unlimited opportunities for scientific mind-play, breaking or exceeding the physical boundaries of actual scientific experimentation. In the SLR, a student examines real data produced in actual experimentation by scientists working in the real world. Unhampered by physical constraints, the SLR student researcher can take that newfound data into his brain to play with it—mentally picking it up, looking at and toying with its different aspects, and using the data in ways unconstrained by formal scientific protocol. Given the right guidance, students researching the SLR begin to play with ideas that were formerly beyond the student's grasp. This mental play is metaphysical and creative, producing scientific thought and building deeper understanding of the subject being researched.

What follows is a lesson-by-lesson guide to teaching science students how to research and write a SLR in American Psychological Association (APA) style. This class of paper is often assigned to undergraduate students in their first years of college and provides a basis for gaining a broad overview of current research in scientific and social science fields. For students, the SLR is a lesson in real-life problem solving, allowing the student to learn how the scientist takes control of a real-life inquiry and introducing research skills to handle real-life scientific questions and studies. The individual workshops are organized around distinct lessons, each teaching specific skills and incorporating content needed to complete the project. Each workshop contains an overview, a workshop plan, and student handout(s). Assessment rubrics are included in seven workshops. Throughout the book, comments are included from collaborating science teachers and participating students about the purpose of the lesson and its impact on the student's scientific understanding.

This SLR unit presents the opportunity to integrate and showcase a modern model for education, in which the collaborating science teacher and librarian serve as content and process guides and the student exhibits mastery of the research topic. The unit utilizes real-life science in the form of peer-reviewed journal studies and permits the student the choice of subject, based upon the student's own research question. This serves to empower the student, whose use of critical-thinking skills and development of a new perspective are enhanced by the personal exploration undertaken.

Students, as well as the librarian and subject teacher, will encounter many challenges while engaging in this unit. Little about the research, material, or research paper protocol is familiar. But the 18 guided inquiry workshops, which are provided, allow students to undertake hard work, aided each step of the way. Student handouts and workshops permit each student researcher to try out a particular research skill under the direct tutelage of the teacher and librarian. No student is ever abandoned to figure it out alone. Many students comment upon completion of the SLR that, although the paper was difficult, it was satisfying. The students then feel quite capable of college-level work.

The long-term success of teaching the SLR rests with solid results and continuing student enthusiasm. Three factors provide evidence of such success: data gathered in school, learning gains of individual students, and external interest garnered for the project.

Each year librarians gather the research folders of the students and place the SLRs in binders. To the teachers, administrators, and visiting parents, the completed science papers generally represent all the data needed. However, librarians also informally survey returning alumni to determine the usefulness of the SLR unit. Librarians collect notes and e-mails from the alumni and share these comments with incoming students, their parents, and newly participating teachers. Students often return during or after their freshman college year with thanks for being taught how to write a SLR which is similar to a college paper.

Science teachers regularly comment on the increased seriousness of purpose and understanding apparent in students who have completed a SLR, especially those who were not particularly interested in science as a discipline. Returning alumni are quick to point out that the skills for writing a SLR are not shared by most members of their college classes during freshman year. Alumni frequently inform librarians that they garner high marks on such college papers. The learning gained by individual students is best portrayed by student acknowledgement that the SLR represents preparation for college, introduction to real-life situations, a strategy for understanding scientific problem solving, and perhaps most importantly, an extended, guided lesson in disciplined thinking.

Outside interest in the SLR has been generated through a pilot study (Kuhlthau & Todd, 2007d) undertaken by Rutgers University researchers and recognition by the Center for International Scholarship in School Libraries (CISSL). The librarians and science teachers have made presentations at professional conferences, in national and international symposia, and at New York City teaching professional in-service conferences. Educators from the United States and abroad have visited the school for program orientations. The educators who teach the SLR have the evidence of its success in the students' folders. After teaching just one unit of the SLR, teachers and librarians alike will experience similar evidence of the enthusiasm, critical thinking, and scientific reasoning of their students engaged in this process.

This book is the result of 14 years of collaborations between science teachers and librarians. The intended audience is the science teacher and the librarian who wish to join forces to teach the SLR. We hope that school principals, division heads, curriculum directors, academic librarians, and college professors of lower-level science and social science courses will also find value added in teaching students how to complete a SLR. Please note that, within the text, the words *teacher* and *educator* may mean science content teacher and/or librarian. Finally, and perhaps most importantly, this book is written for the science student who is seeking a guide in the wilderness of scientific information. We hope the workshops offer each of you the assistance and support needed on the journey through real science to new knowledge.

2

The Inarticulated Question: In the Context of the Debate between Content and Process

The greatest enemy of understanding is coverage.
—Howard Gardner

During the last quarter of the 20th century, as information scientists were grappling with how to create computer program interfaces that would allow efficient and more precise search results of larger amounts of digitalized data, Dr. Nicholas Belkin (1980) coined the term "anomalous state of knowledge." This term describes in a few words the human condition of the questioner being in such a state of mind that he does not even know what he does not know.

How, then, can a questioner who is in an anomalous state of knowledge articulate the question? He has an undeveloped question or need to know about something but is unable to articulate what it is he wants to know exactly because he does not know what he does not know, and therefore cannot state with precision what he wants to know. Certainly, most high school students beginning serious research are in the same anomalous state of knowledge.

In more than 15 years of teaching the Guided Inquiry approach to research, the single question often posed by an adult is, "Shouldn't the student be more specific and/or more focused about the topic of research that he/she chooses?" Teachers ask, administrators ask, parents ask, and sometimes even other librarians ask. The answer is, "No, not necessarily." To adopt the Guided Inquiry approach, the high school educator acknowledges the following conditions:

1. Most students have basic knowledge about subject matter, but even at the Advanced Placement (AP) level, they do not have the depth of knowledge to know what it is they do not know.
2. The discipline and skill of independently acquiring an in-depth collection of information about a subject or question of interest are not frequently taught in a standard high school curriculum.

3. The ability to articulate a research question without first remediating the two prior conditions is limited, and thus the student who is told to do a better job articulating a question will often rely upon a helpful adult to articulate a question, but may not even fully comprehend the suggested articulation.

4. Curiosity and wonder which lead to a question that the student cannot fully articulate can be the driving motivational force for a student undertaking a guided inquiry scientific literature review. Thus, to nurture and fulfill the student's curiosity and wonder so as to sustain the research work, an inarticulated question may be acceptable and becomes the foundation of the research.

Within the context of questions about student research and how much class time should be allotted for teaching students how to do research lies a long simmering debate about the nature of modern high school education itself. Is the modern classroom to focus on the activities of teaching and learning content, or should the students and teachers engage in more activities that focus on the process of learning the content? To put it more succinctly, should students learn "a whole bunch of stuff" as the teacher works furiously to cover the entire textbook (as frequently happens, especially in AP classes), or should students learn how to learn and thus be equipped for future content?

The problem with this debate is that it pits content against process, with each side neglecting the other, and refusing to recognize that in the modern information-laden environment of a high school classroom, too much basic content exists to be learned or covered in any given course and much of that content is also swiftly outdated by new, emerging information. Of course, some skeletal fabric of knowledge must provide students with a basis for making meaning out of newer, incoming stimuli. One must know some content to understand newer content.

If the debate between content and process is framed in a less antagonistic or adversarial context, then process and the teaching of process can be viewed as the enhancement of content education. As content becomes more meaningful with the student's engagement in a search process for information, content then enhances further searching and processing of information. This shared pedagogy predicates a meaningful engagement in educational goals and points the way to increased learning opportunities. Content thus becomes the focus of the learning process and an inarticulated question becomes knowable in its articulation and in the response to its articulation.

The end result of guiding a student through an inquiry that begins with an inarticulated question is the student's motivated involvement and interaction with enough in-depth materials to eventually articulate the question he or she is pursuing through the research. That articulation will happen during the research process and not at the beginning of the process.

3

Collaboration for Meaning

Teaching a scientific literature review (SLR), at its heart, requires a well-planned collaboration between the science teacher and the librarian. They each bring a strong and unique perspective to the collaboration. These collaborations are increasing as both disciplines recognize how their individual professional expertise and skill sets enhance the learning experience of the student and add value to the student's scientific research. The results of the collaboration are larger than the sum of the partners.

I was stuck. Three weeks were left in the school year and I was hoping to delve deep into the nature versus nurture controversy with my introductory psychology class. I had taken a copious amount of notes on a myriad of issues surrounding the topic and planned three weeks of intensive lecture-based classes. I envisioned myself as having to be the "know-it-all" on issues ranging from intelligence to birth order to homosexuality. Truthfully, I was overwhelmed as I lacked the time and scientific knowledge base to dig deep into these issues.

In the end, my three week nature-nurture seminar turned into an exercise in frustration for both myself and my class. They did not respond to the daily lectures that lacked student interaction, and I became disheartened as my lessons, while rich in breadth, lacked the needed depth.

What was I to do? Well, off I went to the library to discuss my problem with our sage school librarian. After listening to my tale of woe, my friendly librarian suggested that I consider having the kids become their own experts on a topic pertaining to nature versus nurture. Students becoming experts and knowing more than I do about a psychological topic? How was this to be?

The concept of a scientific literature review was proposed to me and the rest has been a happy history! No longer are my kids disengaged from their learning, no longer is the content of my course lacking depth and no longer am I frustrated. Through collaboration with the library staff, my students have produced startling research on topics meaningful to them as many have used the assignment to better their understanding of themselves and the world around them.

I have also found that true collaboration is only possible if all individuals involved leave their egos at the doorstep. Truthfully, during the research process, I do not have control of my class. I go from "head coach" to research assistant to the library staff. I am no longer the expert in my students' eyes, but instead am a learner as my knowledge on a researched subject is quickly surpassed by that of my students'. If you are unable to utter the words "I don't know" this type of collaboration is not for you, but if your goal is to provide your class with a meaningful research experience you have stumbled upon gold with the contents of this book! (Mike Wendell, psychology teacher, Gill St. Bernard's School, 2008)

When teachers and librarians meet to explore the concept of the SLR unit, two preconditions are discussed that ensure a successful research project of this nature:

1. A willing, formalized collaboration agreement between the science content teacher and the academic librarian.
2. The understanding that this project is a student-centered, guided inquiry–based research project.

Let us first examine the willing, formalized collaboration between the science content teacher and the academic librarian. This collaboration can be quite fruitful, if there is a cooperative effort that includes the following:

1. A teacher and a librarian, who establish a working partnership based upon acknowledged professional credentials and work history, understand that it boils down to the science teacher as the science expert and the librarian as the information search expert. Both are needed to make the collaboration work.
2. An initial decision is made that the collaboration creates a student-centered research project based on a student-originated inquiry and guided by the collaborating teacher and librarian.
3. Because of the open-ended nature of the SLR as a guided inquiry project, both teacher and librarian are accommodating and flexible with the student and with each other.
4. The collaboration is based upon the science teacher's goals. If, for example, the science teacher needs to teach students how to read scientific studies and write a literature review of those studies to demonstrate scientific critical thought, then the librarian respects the teacher's needs and lends information science and research expertise to the teacher and the student. However, the science teacher may request that the librarian co-teach students how to read the studies and write the SLR.
5. The librarian who is willing to extend herself provides extensive information services to the teacher and the student.
6. The collaboration is designed to meet curriculum requirements but, perhaps, in a new and exciting way.
7. The librarian familiarizes himself with enough of the course content to guide the student in the search and to fulfill the course requirements.

8. A team approach is taken for planning, teaching, guiding, and grading, with clearly defined tasks understood. For example, at least two grades are given on the final paper—one is the research grade given by the librarian and the other is the science content grade given by the science teacher. A third assessment, a separate effort grade that is jointly decided by the librarian and the science teacher, may also be given if the collaborators so choose.

9. The collaborators know, from the planning stage, who is responsible for what, particularly in assignment execution and draft corrections.

10. Once the student has produced the SLR, educators share the story of their collaboration with others, analyze the successes, critique the problems, discuss the collaboration, and allow that discussion to become a pedagogical discourse.

The second precondition focuses on the student's need to know and the educator's commitment to guide the student to a deeper knowledge of the topic. Elements needed to fulfill that focus are understood by the collaborating parties. They include:

1. Collaborating educators recognize the primacy of student choice of topic in an inquiry-based project. If, for example, the student is conducting a literature review in biology or psychology class, the biology or psychology teacher will allow the student to research anything pertaining to the course subject regardless of the teacher's preference. Teachers should allow the student enough time to browse for a possible topic choice as well as enough time to berry pick (Bates, 1989) articles in an apparently random fashion to choose among possible information sources and study topics.

2. Teachers and librarians encourage student's ownership (CISSL, 2007) of the research topic from the point of initiation to taking control of information sources and to the acquisition of real, deep knowledge.

3. Educators build into the assignment and research process adequate time for the teacher and librarian to explain each step and for the student to complete different research stages and tasks. This time is best utilized in a workshop format. All 18 suggested workshops are found in Part II of the book and include a teacher overview, workshop plan, student handout(s), and seven assessment rubrics.

4. Teachers and librarians realize that a variety of outcomes can be expected and plan accordingly to provide tutorial assistance to a student who stumbles.

5. The teachers and librarians always indicate to students the introductory nature of the entire assignment and emphasize that students are not expected to produce a perfect paper.

6. Educators encourage the student, upon completion of the assignment, to reflect on what was learned about the scientific topic as well as the entire research process just completed.

7. Teachers design a time for brief student reports to their peers on the research, allowing for peer questions and researcher answers.

When all these elements are agreed upon by both collaborators and responsibilities are shared to meet the two preconditions, the student researcher is rewarded with two guides assisting in tandem for the duration of this student-centered, inquiry-based research project.

This type of collaboration produces both heat and light. The heat the instructor perceives is a renewed appreciation for the teaching capacities and content expertise of the colleague. The light the student perceives is generated during the process of information handling and deep knowledge development.

4

Serving the Individual Student: Addressing Learning Styles and Differences

As soon as they receive the assignment and begin to read its requirements, students realize that this is not a simple research project but one that will demand significant time and attention. A scientific literature review (SLR) is, in the end, a research paper that requires concentration, research, reading, organization, analysis, and writing. Teachers assigning the SLR understand that not all students excel in these academic areas. A key to the success of the SLR project is the student's buy-in of a difficult assignment whose requirements may not fit his or her individual learning style.

Motivation for the work is provided as a by-product of the student's original inquiry question or idea. A kinesthetic learner who is a soccer player may not like reading per se, but will choose to read studies about athletic training or sports psychology. The trick here is to assist a reluctant researcher in finding a topic he values and has a question about. The question becomes the engine that drives the researcher and the research.

Howard Gardner's theory of multiple intelligences (1993), first introduced over 35 years ago, provides a basis for incorporating student inquiry topics into an assignment to conduct and write a SLR. The research question that drives each study is articulated by the student based primarily on two factors: personal interest and student experience, or lack thereof. Both these factors are influenced by how the student learns and the types of information the student likes to learn about—the same influences highlighted in Gardner's theory of multiple intelligences.

In our experience, multiple intelligences often influence student inquiry. One former student, for example, was a gifted athlete—a runner—and chose to research the physical qualities, skills, and talents that might be possessed by world-class long-distance runners, particularly those from African countries. In other words, his life skills, intelligence, and interests were motivating his science research. Another student, whose interpersonal skills and intelligence were quite apparent, chose to research teenage relationships because she wanted to know how boys related to girls and what made boys act in certain ways. Her research in psychology quickly took on biological underpinnings, motivating further summer research and reading in the physiological and behavioral sciences.

Just as it should be acknowledged that learning styles often influence the student's choice of inquiry, learning differences must also be taken into consideration. One recent student chose the topic of diabetes, not because he was intrinsically interested in the subject, but because his parent was a diabetic. While he gathered information and data, he, like many other students, had concerns about the depth and difficulty of the material—it was not the kind of material he was comfortable handling. With some tutorial assistance, he made his way through the material and produced his literature review relying on specific quotations from the literature to provide the detail as well as more generalized summary notes that he had paraphrased. His treatment of the data was precisely reportorial. His analysis focused on specific points and did not make generalizations or inferences. He completed his review with great success and a budding realization that with hard work real science could be understandable and within reach.

Gill St. Bernard's offers first and second place awards for outstanding papers in psychology, biology, chemistry, physics, cancer research, and interdisciplinary research. These prizes are sponsored by Morristown Memorial Hospital and the Paul Nardoni Foundation. The diabetes research won the student an award. His comments, when asked to describe his prize-winning SLR, were poignant:

> I did my project on diabetes mainly because of my mom. I was curious to find out more for her benefit—and for mine. I wanted to find out about new medicines to help her. She gives herself an insulin shot 4–7 times a day. The project made me realize what she has to go through—how hard it is to live with a life-long disease and all the complications that come along.
>
> The process was hard. I realized I didn't really want to do all this work. After researching I realized what she goes through. I wasn't just doing a project. . . . It became interesting when I saw how hard it is to live with this disease. I felt relief after I finished it. I had a whole new knowledge. I look at my mom differently. I try to help her out more. . . . I felt shocked when I got a prize! Once I started getting into the project I really wanted to win the research prize— even though some people laughed at me and said "You can't win it,"—I knew I could. (Andrew Gunst, student, Gill St. Bernard's School, 2007)

When an assignment is given to a broad and diverse group of students, the teacher and librarian should be prepared to employ multiple pedagogical approaches within one class population. Those approaches, as Kuhlthau (2004) noted, are applied at different times with different students in what she calls "zones of intervention." Basically, the educator meets the student at a point in the Information Search Process (ISP) when the student needs help or does not know what to do next.

Professor Carol Kuhlthau's (1991, 1995; Kuhlthau, Maniotes, & Caspari, 2007, 2012) groundbreaking research and continued scholarship on the ISP describe the actions and responses people experience when conducting research. The ISP has illuminated the SLR project since the program was first designed in 1999. One of the most profound aspects of Dr. Kuhlthau's work is the broad application of her findings. Other

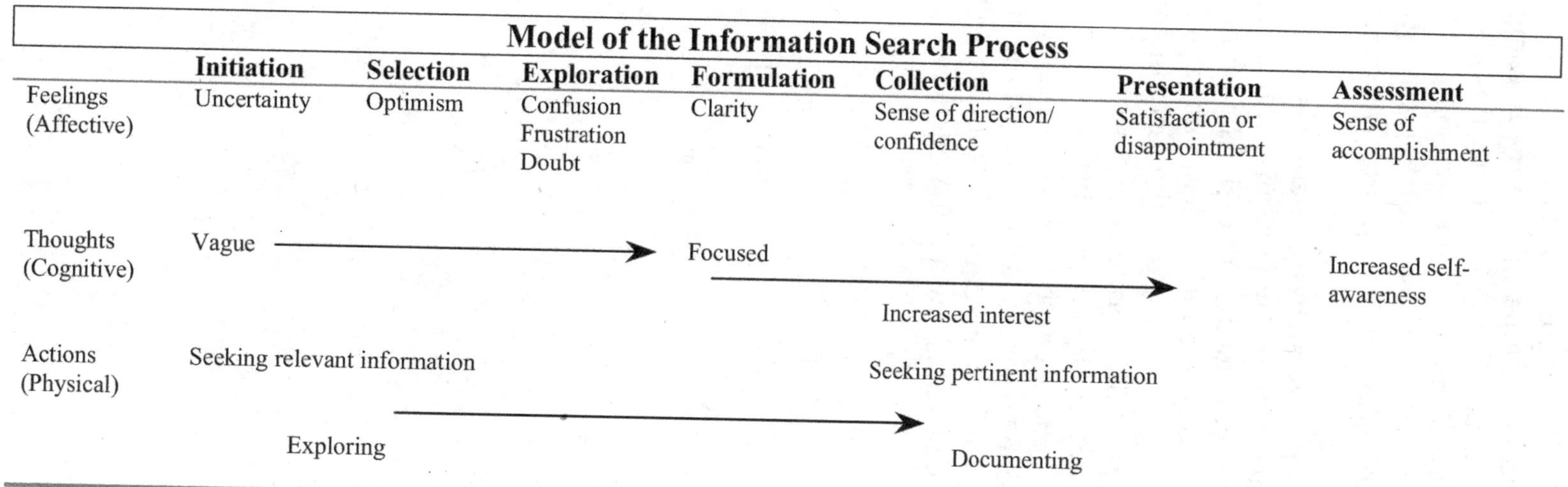

Model of the Information Search Process

	Initiation	Selection	Exploration	Formulation	Collection	Presentation	Assessment
Feelings (Affective)	Uncertainty	Optimism	Confusion Frustration Doubt	Clarity	Sense of direction/ confidence	Satisfaction or disappointment	Sense of accomplishment
Thoughts (Cognitive)	Vague ————————————→			Focused			
				Increased interest			Increased self-awareness
Actions (Physical)	Seeking relevant information —————————————————————→				Seeking pertinent information ————————————————————→		
	Exploring				Documenting		

Figure 4.1 Model of the Information Search Process

Source: Kuhlthau, *Guided Inquiry* (2007), p. 19.

researchers have shown the ISP description to be the same for people of different ages, occupations, and situations in life. See Figure 4.1 for the ISP model.

As noted, different tasks and skills build upon already completed tasks and skills that were previously introduced. Scaffolding or building this assignment level by level (Eick, Meadows, & Balkcom, 2005; Ripton, 1998; Rosenshine & Meister, 1992) permits the teacher and librarian to constantly assess student learning and provide the student with the tutorial assistance necessary for meeting his or her learning styles and differences.

Scaffolding as a means to organize an assignment has been practiced by teachers for several decades but is now more formally recognized. It also serves as a piecemeal puzzle to reduce a seemingly unmanageable, oversized assignment into manageable tasks that, once accomplished, encourage the student and provide motivation for the next task. The student is constantly informed that the assignment, taken as a whole, is challenging and different from any other formerly experienced, *but* each step is taught in a workshop with a hands-on approach, during which direct assistance can be offered to anyone. The student is reminded that each task is doable and that some are actually easy. Having a hard time with one task does not mean that the student will experience difficulty with another. Help is always available as teachers and librarians guide the students through the SLR. The student is never left alone to wander through the information wilderness.

5

Research
Project Assessment

For the educator, correcting the student's first draft is, perhaps, the most labor-intensive aspect of the entire assignment. To allow the educator enough time to correct the first draft of the student's literature review, it should reach the teacher's desk 10–12 weeks after the initial assignment has been given to the student and 2–3 weeks before the final draft is due. Expect the worst, for chances are that some papers will be ugly at best. On the other hand, the teacher or librarian might be pleasantly surprised at the depth of the student's work.

Because this is both an introductory assignment and a new research/presentation process, student drafts will require significant corrections and reminders that must be addressed prior to a final paper being produced. An assessment consisting of correcting each section of the first draft and assigning a pre-grade works well for this project. Pre-grading serves two purposes: (1) It provides the student with a nonbinding assessment that suggests concrete changes and recommendations for additions or subtractions while it maintains a position of positive feedback. (2) It provides the teacher with an already established perspective for grading the final report. When reading several dozen of these rather intricately written presentations of research, the teacher does not have to begin at square one with each paper to determine the final grade, but may compare the final draft to an already corrected and educator-annotated first draft.

Pre-grading can be accomplished by the librarian who is familiar with the research process. The students should be informed, before they submit their first drafts, to expect quite a few corrections. The correcting process serves as an editing process for grammar, citations, and style, as well as a reality check for the research content.

It is important for the teacher and librarian to remember that the draft represents a first-time attempt for the student in a possible lifetime of scientific reviews or other research efforts. The student cannot be expected to hand in a precisely written, beautifully edited, and stylistically correct paper initially. The first draft serves as a prime teachable moment for corrections, reminders, and examination of the comprehensiveness of content. These corrections and reminders include the following categories necessary for a successful paper:

1. Spelling
2. Grammar

3. Citation placement and format
4. Paragraphs
5. Paraphrasing and quotations
6. Introduction that makes sense and piques interest
7. Content that is presented in a scientific manner
8. Connections that are made between studies
9. Analysis that includes the student's critical thoughts
10. Title that accurately depicts research
11. Abstract that succinctly describes research question, lists results of studies found, and indicates analysis of studies
12. Paper is presented in the American Psychological Association (APA) style
13. Research folder and copies of *all* documents of research are presented
14. Reference list format

Before preparing the first draft, the student should be instructed to utilize the current APA style manual in print or online to prepare the first and final drafts. The teacher and librarian correcting the drafts should have a working familiarity with the APA style as well as a copy of the APA manual for easy reference during the corrections and pre-grading process.

The student is informed that *if* the corrections suggested in the first draft are not made in subsequent drafts, the teacher reserves the right to give a lower grade than the pre-grade shown on the paper. On the other hand, if the suggested corrections are made, the pre-grade for each section will represent the *lowest* numerical grade that the student will receive on the final draft. If corrections are made and more precise information is added in the final draft, a student may receive a final grade on that section that is higher than the pre-grade. The student is informed that teacher corrections will take an average of two to three weeks for a large class and that papers are corrected on a first come, first corrected basis.

Each section earns an established numerical point (e.g., 10), if all criteria are met and corrections are made as a result of the pre-grading process. In the case of those students who excel in any given section, extra credit points may be given during the pre-grading process. The correcting teacher and librarian should also, in each section, provide explanatory comments to guide the student from the first draft to the final paper. Pre-grading is only done to assess form and research. Content is generally noted for cohesion and clarity but not pre-graded, although the lack of content will be noted. This, however, can become another option in the assessment process. Students are also encouraged to speak to both content teacher and librarian as questions arise. Content teachers are best equipped to assess content coverage and suggest content options, while librarians can dispense research tactics and citation guidance.

Because, overall, this assignment introduces skills and is never intended to be a mastery-of-skills assignment, an emphasis is placed on student effort and assignment completion. Each section is assessed to determine if the student dealt with the assignment in a conscientious manner and attempted to fulfill all the requirements of that section of the paper. For example, on pre-grading the introduction section, the librarian will assess whether the student has a strong introductory statement and will look at the "hook" to see if it accurately ties into the topic being researched.

The librarian will count the number of different sources of information used in this section to determine if the sources meet the criteria set in the initial assignment and will also look at the quality of the source information and examine the contents' citations to be sure they are correctly placed and listed. The correcting librarian will review information summaries, paraphrasing, and quotations to determine if the citations are properly handled. In addition, the librarian will determine that the information is suited to the research topic and that the introduction flows smoothly; only then will the librarian grade for coverage and effort. The draft is not pre-graded for excellence as much as it is pre-graded for completion of assigned tasks.

Each final paper is at least double graded. The grade given by the content teacher assesses the scientific question addressed by the student and determines the quality of the student's scientific materials, presentation, and analysis. The second, equally weighted grade is given by the librarian. That grade, which is pre-graded on the draft, assesses quality, quantity, depth and breadth of the student's research, and the quality of the student's report of the research found. This second research grade is incorporated into the science course grade. A possible third grade for effort can be assessed by both educators if so desired.

The key to facilitate assessment of the scientific literature review (SLR) is the student's research folder. This folder is a necessary information management tool for each student and an assessment tool for the correcting teacher and librarian. The librarian passes out a glossy, colored, sturdy, two-pocketed research folder to each student researcher. The student may not leave class without writing his or her name and class on a white label attached to the folder. When a student hands in the first draft, the research folder, containing printouts or copies of all pertinent information used and cited in the literature review, must be handed in as well. The folder should include copies of all general press articles (including citation information) and copies of all database printouts of peer-reviewed scientific studies used in the literature review, as well as copies of any book chapters or journal studies found in other print media. The student should be informed that studies can be found in both print and electronic media. The teacher and librarian, therefore, have access to *all* the literature being utilized and reviewed in the paper. This provides the option of cross-checking for clarity and accounting for citations made by the student.

One does not have to second guess the student if plagiarism is suspected. Conversely, if the student capably handles some borrowed information, the teacher can use the source to suggest more in-depth interpretation or alternate sources for further research. In addition, every handout provided in the 18 student workshops is included in the folder. These materials in the folder are the basis of the student's accountability to the scientific research. All student-used borrowed information (quotations as well as material that has been paraphrased or summarized) can be found within the folder and thus allows the teacher or another reader to replicate the literature review. The documents provide the basis for scientific accountability within the student's SLR.

By maintaining the folder, the student is taught responsibility for the sources utilized and is able to readily produce all information used. The student learns organizational skills and documentary/citation responsibilities as well. The folder, because it is turned in with the drafts and final paper, is at the grader's fingertips for consultation. The onus is off the educator to discern the student's progress and to discover the student's sources. By referring to the folder, the teacher may check each and every source to be certain of the veracity of the student's statements and the accountability of the research.

6

Replication and Flexibility Squared

Science depends upon replication, in the broader sense, to keep itself honest. Education in a classroom setting requires flexibility to keep students involved. This chapter examines two applications of the concepts of replication and flexibility.

The question is, can this assignment, originated and executed in a small private college-preparatory high school in New Jersey, be replicated in other curricula and settings? The answer is yes, but with a certain amount of flexibility. The strength of this approach to teaching the scientific literature review (SLR) is its detailed hands-on methodology, which we have titled the *Student Workshops*. These workshops, delivered in a collaboration between the science teacher and the librarian with the assistance of a library aide (resource guide), depend upon a guided student inquiry-based process, one in which the student chooses a topic and the teacher and librarian act as guides.

Replication 1—Repeating the assignment in your setting:

In the years of teaching this project to hundreds of students of varying capabilities—from a slow learner to a top-of-the-class, from English as a second language (ESL) to attention-deficit disorder (ADD) students, from a kinesthetic learner to a science whiz, and many in between—the lessons have been replicated and applied. Some students, quite obviously, demand more tutorials. They are often not only the slower students, but also the brighter students, who choose harder, more demanding material. Replication is focused on repeating the project in a way that is manageable for the school, the teacher, and especially the students. Changes in the project could involve scaling back the number of articles and studies and expanding the time frame of the assignment to an entire semester or reducing the requirements or length of the paper. One teacher might assign a team or group to one inquiry/research question and paper, while another might design a semester-long elective course in scientific research and provide after-school tutorials. Adjusting the assignment to a particular setting, schedule, or circumstance requires flexibility from those undertaking this collaboration, but it can be done.

Replication of this project is possible with the support of school administrators, with defined lines of communication between educators, and with careful planning and execution of workshops. Flexibility allows educators the ability to make this project their own and permits students the possibility of growing with the work required of them.

Replication 2—Introducing the concept of scientific replication to students:

Replication is the cornerstone of the scientific method and a chief means by which a scientist is held responsible for research. If another scientist wishes to replicate or repeat the research, the study, which has been written into a formal report and published (generally after having been peer reviewed), serves as the blueprint for replication. The replicating scientist understands that if the methodology can be precisely repeated, the results of the research should also be repeated.

A formal report of the research (the study) is issued and published to share with the scientific world. Most often, this report is published in a paper-based or online journal associated with a scientific society. Examples of such journals are:

- *Science*
- *Nature*
- *The Journal of Forensic Psychiatry & Psychology*
- *The International Journal of Medical Sciences*
- *Physics Today*
- *American Journal of Public Health*

The study should be written in a clear and complete manner so that another scientist might replicate it. The methodology or procedures section of the study should describe precisely the scientific work that is the basis of the report: what was studied; how much was studied; where and when the study occurred; what procedures were employed for the study; what questions were asked within the study; what instruments, measurements, and standards were used to collect and gauge the data of the study; and how the data were analyzed once they were collected.

Once the methodology section is complete, turn to the results of research section for a description of what was found in the study. If one were to replicate a study precisely, then the second iteration of that study—the replication—should produce the same research results as the original. The data from the replication should ideally match the data from the original study. In a replicated study, although the data should be similar if not the same as in the initial study, the analysis of that data could be different. This may be the result of different perspectives or training on the part of the replicating scientist. This process of reporting and replication provides the basis for scientific honesty and accountability in research.

A SLR provides an excellent means to practice replication. Within the methodology, and reiterated in the references, is a listing of all journals searched with precise, reported search terms. The span of publication time is also given and the names of databases accessed for entrée to those journals are listed, as are the access dates for those databases and/or the Digital Object Identifier (DOI) number, which identifies each distinct document found. With all this information provided in the methodology, the teacher or another student should be able to replicate the student researcher's study and find the same articles. If all else failed, the teacher could reproduce the student's search by finding the copies of all articles used that have been placed within the student's research folder.

Flexibility 1—Teacher flexibility in the assignment:

This process of reporting on research calls for teacher flexibility in the assignment. With the employment of a SLR assignment to introduce students to scientific writing, a note of caution must be sounded. This assignment is a very different exercise for most students. When employing it as an introduction to higher-level science writing, the teacher must exercise a certain amount of flexibility in four distinct areas. These areas include:

1. *Source of information in study*—The assignment requires that a certain number of peer-reviewed studies having been published within the last five years be examined and reviewed. An exception can be made to include an older classical study that points the way to other newer studies. The teacher may exercise flexibility and lift the five-year source limitation, if the student has chosen an obscure topic that has not been studied in the past five years. In some cases, such as research into quantum physics, the requirement of peer-reviewed studies must be lifted to include published or unpublished white papers (theoretical papers) or conference presentations that examine the issue but have not been peer reviewed or may not report actual research completed. These papers can be obtained online on scholarly or university websites. Students may find references to them in conference proceedings or news reports. Occasionally, a student may need to track down such a paper. It is the responsibility of the student (sometimes with help) to provide evidence of the authority of the source and authorship of such a paper.

2. *Breadth of information*—In a professional SLR, the scientist-author is trained, is experienced in scientific research, and has a working knowledge of scientific writing. The scientist will conduct a much more extensive, specific, and detailed search for literature to review. The search may also reflect certain perspectives or bias on the part of the scientist. The resulting paper will be quite focused. For the neophyte student researcher, the literature review is a hit-or-miss proposition. The student usually knows very little about the topic and is simply being introduced to the research process. In the words of Rutgers University's information scientist, Nicholas Belkin (1980), the student is in an "anomalous state of knowledge." The student does not even know what he does not know. The student's search will be limited to a small search vocabulary and will be self-limited by the amount of interest in the subject and a lack of expertise. The neophyte researcher has to plow through some tough research material in a strange format. Interest is, therefore, necessary to ensure student incentive. Ironically, although just a few studies are used in each literature review and are generally limited in length and depth by the reader's lack of expertise, the neophyte student will probably (quite by accident and

because of a lack of discrimination) choose a sufficiently broad range of papers to produce a balanced, albeit small, review.

3. *Depth of information*—A third situation requiring teacher flexibility is the depth, or lack thereof, of student knowledge, and from that base, the depth of information the student is able to glean from each study he reads. For example, in any particular study, a neophyte student researcher can read and comprehend most of the entire introduction to the study. That same beginner student researcher will read and understand some or most of the methodology of a study. But the results of the research and analysis sections may require more work and teacher aids, such as a science reference work, science textbook, or discussion with the science teacher. Perhaps the student has never been exposed to statistics or high-level mathematics. Therefore, the methodology, results, and analysis sections may include both statistics and higher level mathematics. The teacher should encourage the student to choose studies that are easier to understand and to seek teacher and librarian assistance and tutorials with studies where the information seems too deep or intimidating. Few students complete a literature review and understand all the information encountered. But then, few well-educated adults thoroughly understand all the new information they first encounter, either.

4. *Analysis of information*—Even within studies completed by professional scientists, the replication of research portrayed in the study often ends in the results of research section. The replicating scientist may use the results to create a new and different analysis based upon his own specialized knowledge, scientific perspective, and newly available information from other scholarship. The student should be reminded that science builds upon itself. What one scientist finds and analyzes, another scientist uses to create new ideas and seek further data, more information, and more analysis. Simplicity is the rule for a novice researcher who is reading a piece of scientific literature and discerning information from it. The novice must compare or contrast that information to information from other pieces of scientific literature. This is not an easy task! The teacher should look for clear-cut, simple comparisons and not for complicated models or complex technically supported arguments. It is important to recall in the analysis of results section that the student exercises critical thinking skills and supports ideas with clear newfound examples from the data of the studies. In addition, the student should be encouraged to note apparent omissions and errors made in the original studies and project, extrapolate, or imagine the direction of future studies. The teachers should take care to require full citation of all data in the American Psychological Association (APA) style.

Flexibility 2—Dealing with the student's needs:

The guided inquiry-based approach to the SLR provides the foundation for continued student interest and the motivation to push ahead. It is, however, a labor-intensive project for all involved—the student, teacher, and librarian—and demands extensive time and effort from each. This assignment introduces a set of skills that, it can be assumed, are very new to the student who has never had to write a literature review. One can safely assume that few, if any, high school students have ever read a SLR and probably none can define or describe the purpose and function of the SLR.

Such an assignment is brand new to the student and, in fact, may be brand new to the teacher as well. This novelty underscores the introductory nature of the lessons. The teaching team is initiating the skills. The teaching team is neither reinforcing nor perfecting the skills, but instead is nurturing new skills in young or inexperienced science students. Thus, the teacher and librarian are guides for the student's journey through new information territories to complete a first-ever SLR. Such a strategy calls for flexibility. One can tweak the original assignment and scale it down to save class time and student effort. One can also require a literature review that uses only four studies and eliminate the lesson on abstracts. The librarian can omit the Reference List if necessary, but it is critical to insist that the student provide citations in the text and include all studies in the research folder. One can introduce and teach a leaner version of the unit.

But first, stop and ask whether this 12-week-long project will provide more of an opportunity for students to encounter authentic science and grapple with a real-world scientific question that is important to the student. Consider if the exercise exposes the student to the process and content of science in a meaningful way that is different from lectures, note taking, controlled experiments, lab reports, and testing. Better yet, just go ahead and take the risk. Give the assignment, teach the workshops, and then ask the student what the experience has been for some very real answers!

The teacher practicum is now complete. In Part II of the book, educators will find all materials necessary to begin and carry out a unit of researching and writing a scientific literature review (SLR). Each of the 18 following workshops provides a brief overview of the workshop, workshop plan, and handouts for the students. Seven workshops that produce portions of the SLR that are graded also include a rubric for assessment.

Finally, interspersed throughout the book are comments of science teachers who have taught the SLR at Gill St. Bernard's School and the alumni who have participated in the SLR workshops. For those educators who love science and teaching, the results of this student-centered, inquiry-based unit are a joy to behold!

Hi Mrs. Schmidt,

I just want to send a quick email to thank you for teaching me how to research and write an academic paper. Recently, I had to submit an abstract and bibliography to a professor to get approved before I started my final paper. The next day in class she lectured all of us on our inadequate research and incorrectly done bibliographies, and told us she was disappointed in the "obvious gap in our education". Today, I received her comments on my assignment, where she complimented my organizational and research skills and told me that I was the only student in class with a properly done bibliography. I learned all of these skills from you so I wanted to give you the thanks you deserve for teaching me this important lesson. Learning how to do a proper research paper is a skill that every student needs when moving on to higher level education, and even though I may not have realized all of that at the time, I'm very thankful that I know it now.

I hope you've been having a wonderful year.

Sophie Ilaria, 2013
Gill St. Bernard's Alumna, 2012

Mrs. Schmidt,

I hope that you had a great year at Gill! I just wanted to send you an email to thank you for all that you taught me over the years. Today was my third day working as a researcher with a professor in the Astronomy Department here at Penn State. On my first day, the professor gave me a large stack of papers written by other professors in the field, and I was to read the papers and analyze the data that they presented. For the first two days I read the papers and realized that there were some gaps in the data that would affect our research in the coming weeks. I went to her to discuss this, and she was extremely impressed that I was able to come up with the conclusions that I did. When she asked if I had done any previous research, I was proud to say that I had learned everything from you. You always told me that the research we did Junior year would help me in the future, and I am happy to say that you were right! Once again, thank you for everything. I probably wouldn't have this research position if it wasn't for you.

Sydney Sherman, 2012
Gill St. Bernard's Alumna, 2011

Part II

Student Workshops

Research in the Initiation Stage of the Information Search Process

Workshop 1: The Benefits of a Scientific Literature Review
Workshop 2: The Student's Assignment Begins
Workshop 3: Making It Meaningful: Browsing Databases/Finding Information
Workshop 4: Creating and Organizing the Research File

The Teaching Team for the 18 structured workshops will include three educational guides. They are: the content or classroom teacher, the librarian, and a third resource guide who will be either a teacher/library aide or a content expert depending upon the particular workshop being conducted.

While the Initiation Stage contains four workshops, the teacher and librarian are encouraged to allow other additional unstructured class workshop times, particularly after the syllabus has been distributed and the active involvement of each student has begun. Students need time to examine introductory materials from specialized encyclopedias, guides, and manuals in the reference section of the library. They may wish to employ a Google search or discuss possibilities with other students, teacher, or librarians. In-class readings of materials, video viewing, photographic content viewing, or interaction with a content teacher should be permitted as students dip their toes into the research process.

The roles of librarian and teacher include field guide in the library, reference guide for the initial materials, and, perhaps most importantly, time management guide as the adults circulate among the new scholars to help them stay on task and not waste valuable academic time.

There are seven stages of the Information Search Process, from initiation through to evaluation. (See the ISP model on page 19 in **Teacher's Practicum.**) Three experiences accompany each stage: (1) Feelings about the project, (2) thoughts about the information, and (3) activities undertaken while researching information. The students now begin the first stage: Initiation.

Workshop 1

The Benefits of a Scientific Literature Review

Overview

The Scientific Literature Review increases the student's focus and provides the student with an appreciation for the sciences and thus an increase in his motivation to learn. The inquiry-based nature and structure of this project encourages deep understanding and deep knowledge in the sciences. The benefits of this project go beyond the sciences because the research skills students acquire can be used in many subject areas. (Laurence Bostian, Physics Teacher, Gill St. Bernard's School, 2007)

The goal of this introductory workshop is for the student to understand the role of a scientific literature review (SLR) in the world of science. Few students are familiar with the concept of a SLR and few can answer the following questions: What is scientific literature? How do scientists report their studies? What is the purpose of writing a research paper that reviews the literature about a scientific topic?

Before reviewing the assignment to write a research paper—the SLR—the student should be informed that the body of his or her paper will consist of two main sections. The first section is an introduction to the topic of the study that contains information garnered from the popular (general) press. The second section is the report and analysis of scientific studies recently published about a chosen topic. At least six articles from sources such as newspapers, popular magazines, television documentaries, film, photographic documents, and interviews must be used for the Introduction. At least six scientific studies published in peer-reviewed (PR) scientific journals must be used for the rest of the paper (the literature review portion of the paper). Both popular-press articles and PR studies must have been published within the last five years.

To explain the benefits of the SLR to a student who has probably never even read one, the teacher must accomplish three objectives:

1. Review the scientific method.
2. Explore new scientific questions and how these questions lead to new scientific knowledge (Edelman, 1998), which is then shared by dissemination through an information hierarchy that builds up, then flows down.

3. Emphasize that the type of writing the SLR requires is the means by which the scientific community reports and disseminates its work.

Each of the three tasks is relatively simple to accomplish.

The first task is to review the scientific method by first asking students to explain how scientific information is gathered:

A. By laboratory experimentation
B. By field analysis
C. By observation
D. By data collection
E. By interview or *one-on-one* questions/responses
F. By questionnaires or study instruments
G. By sample collection
H. By case study

- Ask students why information is gathered and if a research question is based on prior knowledge or earlier observations.
- Lead students through the acknowledged protocol of the trained scientists who undertake research by using the scientific method. This protocol (Postlethwait & Hopson, 2003) includes:

  - Asking a question
  - Proposing a hypothesis
  - Making a prediction
  - Testing the prediction
  - Coming to a conclusion

Be sure to observe that the hypothesis is difficult to frame for the neophyte researcher. Therefore, the student is not expected to frame a hypothesis. A research question or idea, rather than a specific hypothesis, can guide the student though a literature review of a chosen topic.

Some examples of research questions that students recently asked include:

1. What are the underlying causes and experimental treatments for Hutchinson-Giford Progeria Syndrome?
2. What are the diagnostic methods and determining factors of Alzheimer's disease?
3. What are the neurological and biological factors of sleep disorders?
4. What is Autism Spectrum Disorder in males?
5. What are the influences of Synesthesia in the perception of reality?
6. Does the media influence eating disorders?
7. What are the cognitive effects on learning and treatments for dyslexia?
8. What are the effects of and interference with life quality of antiepileptic treatments?
9. What are the effects of telomere length and telomerase production in aging?
10. What is the manifestation and prevention of head trauma in the sport of hockey?

11. What are the physiological effects of birth order on sibling behavior?
12. What are the effects of Type-1 and Type-2 diabetes on youth?
13. What is a play-based learning approach in early childhood education?
14. Is equine-assisted therapy for handicapped people effective?
15. What are the patterns of adolescent depression and suicide?
16. What are motivational influences and psychological skills within athletes?
17. What factors of aerobic movements cause Medial Tibial Stress Syndrome?
18. What are the effects of music on the human brain?
19. What factors contribute to anxiety?
20. Are Superstring and M Theories related?

The role of the SLR is to expose the reviewing scientist to the past, current, and ongoing research about a subject the scientist is exploring for future research of his or her own. Thus, the literature review can become the a priori stop made before a hypothesis is formulated or it can provide confirmation of an already existing hypothesis. In either case, the SLR provides the scientist with an extended understanding of the topic being reviewed, preventing unnecessary first-person research of a topic already studied while indicating past experiments, results, and analyses.

To borrow and reinterpret a concept employed by Albert Einstein, the SLR enables the prospective scientist to mentally play with a research idea by employing a thought experiment (Ireson, 2005), examining the SLR before actually undertaking his or her own physical experiment. In other words, the student conducts a minds-on experiment unencumbered by physical requirements, equipment, safety regulations, time, manpower, methodologies, data collection, and a lack of antiseptic environments; the SLR places science into the mind of the student. Any subject that science has reported is possible for a student to investigate. The student accustomed to reading, reporting, and analyzing actual scientific literature is actively engaging the world of science and participating in a thought experiment of a unique type, setting the stage for his or her own scientific thinking and future scientific inquiry.

The second task in explaining the benefits of a SLR is to explore how scientific questions (Edelman, 1998) lead to new scientific knowledge. One method of explaining the role of science in developing new knowledge, and then disseminating that new knowledge, is achieved by providing a humorous, fantastic scenario that could happen at any high school on any given day. This scenario illustrates an event which breaks the status quo and provides an example of something new and puzzling which occurs one morning at a small high school. The scenario involves a biology teacher who is well-liked by students and faculty. This is the scenario:

One morning, an ordinary morning at the school, a bus drives onto the campus and out of the bus step 25 living copies of the biology teacher, Michael Stil, who the students have nicknamed "Stil". The twenty-five Stils are all exact replicas and, in fact, one of them is the original Stil. The arrival of the Stils has broken the usual status quo of a school day and something new has occurred. The news event is first circulated among first hand witnesses, who then tell other students of the event which the non-witnesses have not personally experienced. At some point the school newspaper runs the story and the town newspaper or radio station picks up the story. Meanwhile, social media are also noting the story. The questions being asked are, "Who are the 'Stils' and why are they invading the school? What do they want? Is it biology education they want to teach?"

Eventually, a national morning television show sends a reporting crew out to interview the Stils and the students. A behavioral scientist later watches the show and is intrigued by the Stil phenomena. What is the effect, she wonders, of all the Stils upon the student body: are they learning more biology or are they just distracted by so many Stils? She decides to conduct a study of the effects on biology education by 25 Stils in one small high school. Her study (like the studies of most scientists) involves a question, a group studied, and a method of conducting her study. She then finds and analyzes the results and submits her study to a peer-reviewed journal for publication.

If chosen for publication on the basis of the scientific quality of her work, the study then becomes part of the public domain. It is new knowledge which works its way to major media outlet print and online science publications, and eventually to popular media.

This example of new information, instigated by the breaking of the status quo, popularized by media, and then studied by science illustrates the development and the later dissemination of new knowledge. This development of new knowledge is the essence of scientific endeavors.

Science and the accumulation of new knowledge (Edelman, 1988) are the result of a two-way flow of information that begins with something ordinary being interpreted or something seemingly extraordinary happening. The occurrence results in stories (anecdotes) being created and reported. As the anecdotes travel up the information channels, from storytelling to newspaper, magazine, radio, television, Internet, and other mass media, they result in collections of like information that are published in nonscientific books. Scientists, tantalized or curious about the information, begin to analyze what they have encountered and, for one or many reasons, decide to study the phenomena. Applying the scientific method, scientists read whatever they can that is already published, formulate a hypothesis, determine a methodology, gather data, record their results, analyze those results, compile a conclusion, and finally include a reference list of previously published works used and cited in the study. After the study is written, the scientist submits it to a recognized journal that publishes scientific literature in a certain field or subfield of knowledge. The journal can be published in print or digitally or in both formats. Journals are often the publishing voices for professional scientific (membership) associations.

After receiving the manuscript for the study (Edelman, 1998), the journal editor contacts a small number of peer-editing scientists familiar with the subfield of science reported in the study. These peer editors examine the study for its scientific content. They act as scientific judges to determine the accountability and authenticity of the study. They may call for revisions or make suggestions, and eventually they recommend or not recommend publication of the study.

Once a study is published in a scientific journal, it enters the public domain for scientific and nonscientific comment. Certainly, other scientists will read and may comment upon and replicate the study. But newspaper commentators and popular journalists (Edelman, 1998) may report on the study as well, editorializing the study or introducing the information in the popular press and media. Thus, a scientific study, held up to the highest scientific scrutiny by peer review before scientific journal publication, enters the public nonscientific domain—a common new knowledge to be used by all.

The third task is to emphasize that the type of writing found in the SLR is similar in style and content to the writing that scientists employ to share their research. This task can be easily accomplished by providing students with print journals that contain published studies and assisting students in finding digitally published studies in online databases. The worldwide scientific community's tradition of sharing information is best exemplified through the perusal of multiple electronic databases covering a myriad of subjects. For the newly initiated researcher, nothing surpasses sitting down at a computer, browsing a peer reviewed database collection or printouts, and reading sample studies. Observations may be made that science can build upon itself through the sharing of a study, constructing new meaning, and producing new knowledge for the good of humanity and the world.

At this time, each student should be presented with a sturdy two-pocket folder to contain all handouts. Having been introduced to the SLR as a tool to initiate the creation and dissemination of new scientific knowledge, the students are ready to receive and review their assignment. Students can be reminded that engaging in the SLR will encourage critical thinking as well as prepare them to successfully complete college assignments in the sciences and social sciences. They might be among the few college students who are prepared! All future workshops will alternate in gender reference between male and female. Workshop 2 will be all male references and Workshop 3 will be all female references, and so on.

Workshop 1: The Benefits
of a Scientific Literature Review

Learning Goals: The goal of this workshop is for the student to understand the role of a Scientific Literature Review (SLR) in the world of science.
Location: Library/classroom
Team: Teacher, Librarian, and Resource Guide
Inquiry Unit: This workshop shall provide an introduction to a guided, inquiry-based scientific research and writing project using the syllabus as an example of a plan for learning scholarly research.
Total Time: 50 minutes

Starter Time: 25 minutes	The science teacher will begin by writing on the board the following questions which will be asked of the students and the librarian will lead the discussion after distributing Handout 1: 1. How is scientific knowledge developed? 2. How is it gathered, shared, and evaluated? 3. How do scientists communicate their investigative results to both scientists and nonscientists? 4. How does the scientific method apply to a minds-on science research investigation? 5. How does a simple question lead to scientific research?
Work Time Time: 20 minutes	A news article will be displayed or print versions passed out. This article will be about a current study pertinent to teenage life. Students will read the article. Next, the students will be given examples of studies (which are not terribly complex) to examine each section of the study, read the first paragraph of each section, and discuss with a partner what each study reflects and why the scientist conducted the study. The teaching team will circulate to point out the different sections of the study and answer questions that the individual students might have.
Reflection Time: 5 minutes	The class will discuss that the study is a complex set of information that they probably have never read prior to that day. The librarian will assure students that the entire project will be a joint and supportive exercise in which the students will never be left alone to complete the assignment. There will always be help available and most of each assignment will be initiated and partially completed in the workshop format provided.
Notes	The teaching team may combine **Workshop 1: The Benefits of a Scientific Literature Review** with **Workshop 2: The Student's Assignment Begins**, if time permits.
Common Core Standards	*CCSS.ELA-Literacy.RST.11-12.2*: Determine the central ideas or conclusions of a text; summarize complex concepts, processes, or information presented in a text by paraphrasing them in simpler but still accurate terms. *CCSS.ELA-Literacy.RST.11-12.6*: Analyze the author's purpose in providing an explanation, describing a procedure, or discussing an experiment in a text, identifying important issues that remain unresolved.

From *Teaching the Scientific Literature Review: Collaborative Lessons for Guided Inquiry*, by Randell K. Schmidt, Maureen M. Smyth, and Virginia K. Kowalski. Santa Barbara, CA: Libraries Unlimited. Copyright © 2014.

Handout: The Benefits of a Scientific Literature Review

Why Do I Have to Do This Project?

This year, you will undertake a scientific research project. This project is a Scientific Literature Review (SLR) of your chosen topic, which must be pertinent to the field of information that you are studying within your current science class. Thus, environmental science students choose an environmental subject, psychology students choose a subject about human behavior, chemistry students choose a topic about chemicals or the chemical basis of reality, and so on.

In real life, before a scientist undertakes new research, he or she conducts a literature review to find out what has already been examined about his or her subject and what results have been found. This way, the scientific community gains from new knowledge and individual scientists avoid redundant studies—they do not reinvent the wheel. The subject that you choose to research is expected to be one in which you have some interest but little knowledge. As a matter of fact, should you know nothing at all about the subject, do not fear. You may, in your ignorance, get a broader picture of current research and thinking than if you had both knowledge and a bias based on that knowledge.

However, because you know so little before doing your literature review, you will not have to start this paper with a hypothesis and then give proofs within the body of the paper. You really do not know enough to formulate a hypothesis. Instead, you will review both general press literature found in newspaper articles, popular news magazines, television documentaries, film, or popular culture to determine what, in general, society is saying about your topic, and then the scientific literature to discover what scientists are studying and finding about your topic.

Here is the key to success in your paper: You must access, read, and interpret at least six current (no more than five years old) research studies in scientific PR journals. These articles must be full reports in scientific reporting style, such as the *Publication Manual of the American Psychological Association* (APA), which a scientist or group of scientists has conducted on the topic you have chosen.

In handling this material, you will be exposed to current research in your field of study. Hopefully, you will receive more than one perspective on your topic and you may, in fact, encounter existing controversy about your topic. You will also observe different research methods among your studies and a variety of outcomes. The subjects studied will change from study to study and the questions driving each study may differ greatly. But all this will help you to understand that science is in a state of constant change and that it builds upon previous science, thus portraying such change as an expected result of observation, experimentation, and interpretation of newfound data.

Workshop 2

The Student's Assignment Begins

Overview

The goal of this workshop is the student's review of the overall assignment in which all aspects of the research paper are discussed and the initial brainstorming for a topic begins. The multipage assignment introduces the seven sections of the paper:

1. *Cover Page and Abstract*
2. *Introduction*
3. *Methodology*
4. *Results of Research*
5. *Analysis of Research*
6. *Conclusion*
7. *Reference List*

A good method of illustrating the assignment is to provide each student with a student-produced research file. If one is not available, the teacher can create a mock file of a potential research project containing six general press (GP) articles, six peer-reviewed (PR) studies, and a sample literature review. The lesson then begins with the student looking at each section of a study and reading the first two paragraphs of each section of the sample literature review. Students then examine one published study to see that it reflects a cover page and an abstract, a question driving the study, a group being studied, a method being used to gather information, and a results of research section, as well as an analysis of the results, a brief conclusion, and a reference list. If the teacher has conducted this project at least once, a sample paper can be presented of seven different examples by previous students of the seven sections within the paper.

In the assignment, the student is informed of the time required and difficulty of this kind of research and assured that each research step will be explained in a workshop format. The student is told that such research is accomplished using two types of sources:

1. General press (GP) or popular media sources such as newspapers of note (large city newspapers often staffed with trained science writers or editors), magazines, books, and interviews for the information incorporated into the introduction.

43

2. Scientific studies published in peer-reviewed (PR) scientific journals, both in print and online, for the body of the scientific literature review (SLR).

Again, the student is reassured that these workshops will teach him how to find the best science information sources. The student reads in the assignment how many sources are required for the paper and approximately how long it will take to find and read the required number of studies. Finally, the assignment includes a timeline and a short list of the due dates for sources, drafts, and final paper to be given to the correcting teacher or librarian.

The workshop format of this assignment allows the student to ask questions during the initial assignment reading. The teacher and librarian's presentation of the assignment usually provides some time for brainstorming possible topics the student might research. To that end, the librarian brings to the class two sets of examples of scientific literature. The first set is five or more professionally published studies (including, if possible, a published SLR) for the student to examine, reflecting a variety of topics of different lengths and levels of difficulty. The second set of examples could be previously written student SLRs (if available), and these, too, should reflect a variety and degrees of sophistication and expertise. At the end of the class, the student should be reminded to place the assignment and all future handouts in the research folder to be brought to each class meeting.

The independent scientific research project at Gill St. Bernard's School prepared me for my experiences at Sarah Lawrence College. There I was expected to complete three researched in-depth papers per semester. At first it seemed daunting until I realized I had already been through the process while ensconced within GSB's comfortable library.

Meeting every two weeks with a faculty advisor felt just like meeting with Mrs. Schmidt. I would explain what I had read, why I had read it, and how it worked into the study as a whole. At the end of each meeting I would ask if I was going in the right direction, whether or not what I planned to read next still worked for the paper, and what the professor wanted to see from me next. Invariably in my first year at Sarah Lawrence professors would ask me if I was struggling but I felt confident.

The greatest thing I learned and took from the independent scientific research project at Gill was the ability to be both self-reliant and willing to ask for help. Instead of panicking when I could not find what I was looking for, I set up an appointment with a research librarian. Upon walking into the meeting I knew what I wanted and felt excited for the search. (Elizabeth Barback, graduate, Gill St. Bernard's School, 2007)

Workshop 2: The Student's Assignment Begins

Learning Goals: The goal of this workshop is the student's review of the overall assignment in which all aspects of the research paper are discussed and the initial brainstorming for a topic begins.

Location: Library

Team: Teacher, Librarian, and Resource Guide

Inquiry Unit: This workshop shall provide an introduction to a guided, inquiry-based scientific writing and research project using the syllabus and sample papers as an example of a plan for learning scholarly research.

Total Time: 50 minutes

Starter Time: 15 minutes	Distribute the syllabus, sample studies, and popular magazine's holding scientific articles or, if possible, research folders and sample papers from previous years. Ask students to identify general press (GP) and peer-reviewed (PR) materials. Use Handout 1 to introduce the seven sections of the PR paper. Students should be informed that their SLR will reflect the same organization as a professional study.
Work Time Time: 25 minutes	Individual student volunteers are asked to read descriptions of the seven sections of a sample paper out loud. The teaching team aids students in locating and differentiating GP and PR materials and identifying the individual sections of the paper. The teaching team responds to questions asked by students after each section is reviewed. Use Handout 2: The Assignment Timeline to go over the timeline of the assignment. Use Handout 3: Topic Brainstorming as a brainstorming tool for thoughts on conducting a study.
Reflection Time: 10 minutes	Still in the inquiry community, ask students if there are any questions regarding the syllabus and types of information sources. Based upon what the student has seen today, the teaching team can lead a discussion of possible questions that the students might use to conduct a study, thus beginning the brainstorm process.
Notes	You may combine **Workshop 2: The Student's Assignment Begins** with **Workshop 1: The Benefits of a Scientific Literature Review.** If your class period is longer, you may replace the distribution of student examples with the presentation of one example taken from a professional journal if student examples are unavailable. You may use the internet, Power Point, and so on to display a sample student paper or an actual study.
Common Core Standards	*CCSS.ELA-Literacy.SL.11-12.1c*: Propel conversations by posing and responding to questions that probe reasoning and evidence; ensure a hearing for a full range of positions on a topic or issue; clarify, verify, or challenge ideas and conclusions; and promote divergent and creative perspectives. *CCSS.ELA-Literacy.SL.11-12.6*: Adapt speech to a variety of contexts and tasks, demonstrating a command of formal English when indicated or appropriate.

From *Teaching the Scientific Literature Review: Collaborative Lessons for Guided Inquiry*, by Randell K. Schmidt, Maureen M. Smyth, and Virginia K. Kowalski. Santa Barbara, CA: Libraries Unlimited. Copyright © 2014.

Handout #1: The Assignment: Researching and Writing a Scientific Literature Review

Your assignment is to conduct a scientific literature review of existing scientific research about a topic of your choice that has been approved by your teacher. The requirements of this assignment include:

Topic: Chosen by you on a subject that relates to your science course. The teacher may provide a list of suggested topics. All topics must be approved by the teacher.

Length: 6–10 pages in length depending upon the science course you are taking.

The following is an outline of the sections contained within a scientifically based literature review. In the outline, a brief overview of each section is given. Please refer to the research paper handed to you to see how past students have taken this outline and incorporated it into a paper. Also, please note that you will not simply be handed a worksheet and told to get to work. A workshop, taught by a research librarian and science teacher, will be held to introduce each stage of the process. Your paper will include five sections (in the body) about what you are researching. The five sections include:

I.   *Introduction*—Introduce the guiding question or idea of the paper (subject, problem, controversy, issue).

- Why are you researching and writing the paper?
- What is the world saying about your subject?
- What statement can you make about your guiding question or idea (i.e., where does the world stand or what is the main question or issue)?
- Can you place your idea in the context of the surrounding controversy or in a general context?
- **Length: 1½–2 pages**

II. *Methodology*—Explain how you got your information.

- Include a list of general press sources and texts used in the Introduction to your paper.
- Include a list of peer reviewed scholarly scientific journals that published studies that you used. These studies were written by scientists, reviewed, and approved by peers of the scientist for publication in the journal. The journals are often accessed online in electronic databases.
- **Length: 2–4 paragraphs**

III. *Results of Research*—"Recent research indicates that . . ."

- This section contains your citations and statements about what scientists have said about the question, problem, controversy, or issue.
- Here, you review what the studies have actually revealed.
- Most of the work you do as a science reporter goes here.
- **Length: 2–4 pages**

From *Teaching the Scientific Literature Review: Collaborative Lessons for Guided Inquiry,* by Randell K. Schmidt, Maureen M. Smyth, and Virginia K. Kowalski. Santa Barbara, CA: Libraries Unlimited. Copyright © 2014.

IV. *Analysis of Research*—Discuss and interpret the implications of what you have found.

- These are your ideas and interpretations that compare the studies you have read.
- This is the most intellectual section of the paper. Your own critical thinking is found here.
- Be creative: Look for *patterns, divergences, concepts, connections,* and *contradictions* among the studies you have read.
- Examine studies for omissions or apparent errors.
- Think about the direction future studies might take.
- **Length: 2–4 pages**

V. *Conclusion*—Introduce no new ideas and summarize what you have found in your research and how you analyzed your research. The Conclusion is simply a summary of the previous four sections of the literature review.

- **Length: 2–4 paragraphs**

Specific Requirements of the Assignment Include

Sources: At least 12–16 sources must be used for the SLR. Of these, at least 6–8 of your initial GP sources should contain more introductory material about your topic, and provide you with a working or background knowledge and a vocabulary to begin the search in scholarly journals. Acceptable GP sources for introductory information include, but are not limited to, textbooks, newspapers of note, nonfiction works, articles in reputable (non-gossipy) magazines, documentaries, photographs, interviews, and so on. In addition, at least six scholarly PR scientific journal studies are required. These are studies that describe research that scientists have completed about your selected topic. The 6–8 PR journal studies must be full text studies that explain recent research, that is, a study of your chosen subject. The articles should not be news items, book reviews, or letters to the editor. These journal studies can be accessed through databases online or through hard copy paper journals in research libraries, such as those in a local college or university collection. The school library also may also collect some hard copy journals and subscribes to several databases containing scientific journals online. The librarians will review how to search for the appropriate information in a workshop.

Style and Citations: Your paper will follow American Psychological Association (APA) style, commonly used in scientific publishing. You will be writing what amounts to a publishable article/journal study that can be offered for peer review, and thus judged scientifically worthy or unfit for publication. APA manuals are stocked in the library or found online.

Presentation: Your paper, written and fully cited in the APA style, must contain:

- *Cover Page with Abstract*
- *Introduction*
- *Methodology*
- *Results of Research*
- *Analysis of Research*
- *Conclusion*
- *Reference List*—The references must be attached to your paper and should include *all GP and PR works cited within your paper and contained within your research folder.*

Research Folder: Your research folder should contain a copy of each article and study you used for your literature review. This way, teachers can check for accurate citation of information and proper handling of borrowed materials.

From *Teaching the Scientific Literature Review: Collaborative Lessons for Guided Inquiry,* by Randell K. Schmidt, Maureen M. Smyth, and Virginia K. Kowalski. Santa Barbara, CA: Libraries Unlimited. Copyright © 2014.

Please complete work on time! Due dates are set by each science teacher:

Choose topic   Due Date _____

Show sources   Due Date _____

First Draft   Due Date _____

Final Paper   Due Date _____

This assignment is difficult, so allow at least 15–20 hours of pure research for a successful paper. Prior to accessing PR journal studies, you should read at least six to eight GP articles in textbooks, books, popular magazines, journals, or newspapers either in hard copy or through online databases to have a basis for understanding your subject and to build a vocabulary for searching scientific studies. When you begin the search in PR studies, you will find some studies that are too technical for your understanding. Discard them and use others that are more understandable. You may only use and cite the non–peer reviewed, general press articles in your paper when you discuss the guiding question or idea and the controversy or context surrounding it in the Introduction. This entire project will last approximately 12 weeks.

The final draft is graded on the basis of a maximum of 70 points—10 points per section. The paper should be formatted with:

Cover Page (including Abstract)	10 points
Introduction	10 points
Methodology	10 points
Results of Research	10 points
Analysis of Research	10 points
Conclusion	10 points
Reference List	10 points

Three grades will be awarded a science content grade (70 points maximum), a research grade (70 points maximum), and an effort grade (60 points maximum). All grades will be incorporated into your science course semester grade.

A TIMELINE IS ATTACHED WITH DUE DATES FOR THIS PROJECT (Handout 2: The Assignment Timeline).

Handout #2: The Assignment Timeline

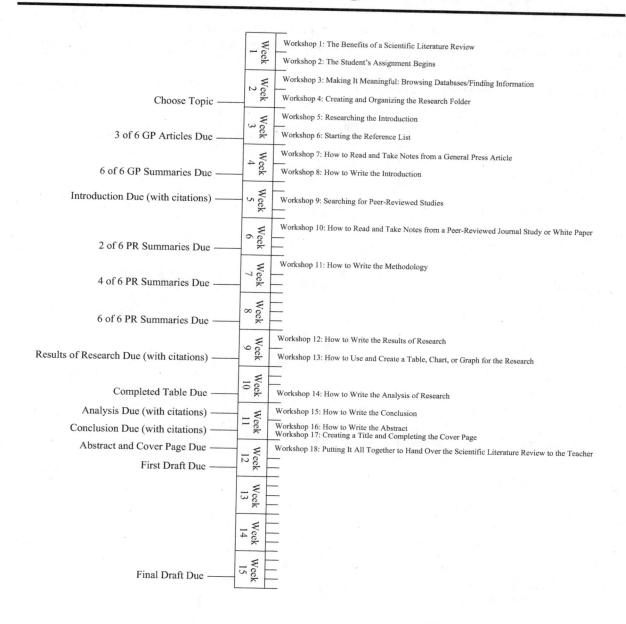

	Week 1	Workshop 1: The Benefits of a Scientific Literature Review
		Workshop 2: The Student's Assignment Begins
Choose Topic	Week 2	Workshop 3: Making It Meaningful: Browsing Databases/Finding Information
		Workshop 4: Creating and Organizing the Research Folder
3 of 6 GP Articles Due	Week 3	Workshop 5: Researching the Introduction
		Workshop 6: Starting the Reference List
6 of 6 GP Summaries Due	Week 4	Workshop 7: How to Read and Take Notes from a General Press Article
		Workshop 8: How to Write the Introduction
Introduction Due (with citations)	Week 5	Workshop 9: Searching for Peer-Reviewed Studies
2 of 6 PR Summaries Due	Week 6	Workshop 10: How to Read and Take Notes from a Peer-Reviewed Journal Study or White Paper
4 of 6 PR Summaries Due	Week 7	Workshop 11: How to Write the Methodology
6 of 6 PR Summaries Due	Week 8	
Results of Research Due (with citations)	Week 9	Workshop 12: How to Write the Results of Research
		Workshop 13: How to Use and Create a Table, Chart, or Graph for the Research
Completed Table Due	Week 10	Workshop 14: How to Write the Analysis of Research
Analysis Due (with citations)	Week 11	Workshop 15: How to Write the Conclusion
Conclusion Due (with citations)		Workshop 16: How to Write the Abstract
		Workshop 17: Creating a Title and Completing the Cover Page
Abstract and Cover Page Due	Week 12	Workshop 18: Putting It All Together to Hand Over the Scientific Literature Review to the Teacher
First Draft Due		
	Week 13	
	Week 14	
Final Draft Due	Week 15	

Handout #3: Topic Brainstorming

Directions: Although you may have a topic in mind, please complete the brainstorming activity. If you have no topic in mind, don't worry! Complete this brainstorming form to get your ideas flowing, which may lead you to a subtopic or may focus or broaden your potential topic.

Fill in one-word or short phrase answers. Be quick and spontaneous. You will not be tied to this, so be honest and thoughtful.

What interests you in general (outside of school, other subjects)?

What science class topics have most interested you?

Why do the science topics interest you? What is important about them?

Is there a possible link or connection between any of those topics?

Which two topics are you most interested in? Are there related narrower or broader topics?

1.

2.

Write your interest in the form of a question. It doesn't have to be perfect!

1.

2.

From *Teaching the Scientific Literature Review: Collaborative Lessons for Guided Inquiry*, by Randell K. Schmidt, Maureen M. Smyth, and Virginia K. Kowalski. Santa Barbara, CA: Libraries Unlimited. Copyright © 2014.

Workshop 3

Making It Meaningful: Browsing Databases/Finding Information

Overview

Databases provide an essential tool for any student writing a research paper. This is particularly true when it comes to writing a scientific literature review (SLR) in which the student needs reliable general press (GP) articles and scientific peer-reviewed (PR) studies to complete the assignment. Teachers can begin the introduction to or review of databases by asking the student if she knows what a database is. It is common to find that a student will recollect using a database in the past or mentions that she has used them infrequently as a resource in a school library setting. Often, the student cannot distinguish between a database and a search engine. Providing the student more in the way of an explanation as to the database's usefulness and appropriateness for this assignment might be indicated at this time. The student may need some hands-on training in the search and uses of specific databases.

Choosing a scientific topic to browse in an electronic database can be a daunting task initially, especially if a student does not have a clue what to look for. A possible solution is readily available in the library print collection of reference works and periodicals. Librarians may begin this lesson by placing specialized encyclopedias on psychology, health, disease and disorders, sports, and environment on the worktables with the students, as well as recent copies of *Scientific American, Psychology Today, Wired*, and *The New York Times* weekly section of *Science Times*. Giving students an opportunity to browse readily available printed material before using the electronic databases allows for inspiration and reduces the stress of finding something immediately online.

The student uses search engines such as Google to find quick answers to her questions. While search engines can provide a wealth of information, she can waste precious time as she finds herself wading through an overabundance of information, much of it commercial and useless, before she finds information that is both helpful and authoritative. Scientific writing requires authority, a characteristic that search engines are not well-designed to provide.

The student and the instructor can feel secure in the knowledge that databases are organized collections, often of edited materials. Using databases, the student can be confident that she is accessing some of the most reliable electronic information available. Databases allow electronic access to hundreds of full text current newspapers, magazines, and PR scientific journals from the convenience of the school library. Subscription databases, which a library purchases, often allow remote access using specific passwords and user information as well.

It might be helpful at this point to provide time for hands-on training or preliminary database browsing for the student, as well as to provide a list of those subscription databases and their passwords that are part of the library's collection. This will allow the student to access and search some of these databases from her home computer. Most school computers allow convenient access to such databases by clicking an icon on the computer desktop or from a drop-down menu selection on the school's homepage. The student, then, simply clicks the icon and selects the desired database or selects one directly from the bookmark menu of the library's homepage.

As the search for information is initiated, the new researcher will be uncertain where to begin and what to look for. This feeling of uncertainty (Kuhlthau, 2004) has been found to be almost universal in the beginning of the Information Search Process. There are two points during the research process where students may feel that beginner's uncertainty:

- When the introductory material search begins
- When the scientific study search is initiated

An antidote to that uncertainty (Allen, 1996) is browsing for information in the databases. This browsing is similar to window-shopping, where students are encouraged to merely look at—not buy—what they find while browsing a database. The student should also be required to look into more than one database for articles about a topic. While browsing, the student should use whatever search term she might already know and read whatever articles are of interest. In reading an article, a student might note the related terms found in the heading section of the article and use those terms to broaden or refine her search for other articles.

The same browsing technique can be applied to the scientific studies searched in the databases, which will yield more definitive alternative search terms and potentially more significant research. Interestingly, through initial and subsequent browsing, the student may experience stimuli and impediments that redirect her research or produce a change in the treatment of her research topic. Browsing may cause the student to refine, change, abandon, or redirect research and, therefore, should be encouraged as she begins the research project.

The database searches for introductory information are extremely useful in developing the student's general knowledge of the scientific topic. They are also useful in providing nonscientific articles for the introductory section of the student's SLR. Accessing GP articles allows the student to see what the world at large is saying about her topic and provides the student with further scientific terms (search vocabulary) to streamline and deepen searching capabilities (e.g., newspaper and magazine).

Searching for GP articles is relatively straightforward. In a basic search through a database, the student types in a search term, checks off full text, indicates a time span of the last five years, and clicks the search button. The researcher is then rewarded with a selection of hits or possibly appropriate articles listed in chronological order of publication. The author, title, source, and date are also clearly indicated. Clicking on the selection provides both a short abstract as well as an entire view of the article. By reading the abstract, the student can quickly determine if the selection may be suitable. If the article seems worthwhile, the student can then read the full text.

Retrieving the scientific studies required for the SLR can be accomplished with either a basic search technique or an advanced search. Some databases, such as *eLibrary*, *Proquest Direct*, and *EBSCO* whose collections include numerous scholarly journals, are more appropriate in searching for scientific studies. Searching for studies is, however, a later activity.

Databases provide basic and advanced searching abilities. Both searching options offer the choice of printing, saving the article electronically, or e-mailing the article. While searching in the advanced mode requires a few more steps, it allows students to zero in and particularize the search in a more sophisticated fashion. Advanced searches can be quickly demonstrated by the librarian.

In the advanced mode, the searcher can be very specific about the information she wants to retrieve. The student can connect several terms together by using and/ or limiters or eliminate unwanted terms by using the not limiter. She should also limit the results, in both the basic and advanced mode, to "full text" for GP articles and scientific studies and "peer-reviewed" for scientific studies. By restricting the search to "peer reviewed" articles, a student will more easily obtain scientific studies. The last step in initiating the search involves setting the publication date to within five years of the date of the assignment. After defining the span of publication, clicking on the search button will retrieve articles listed by title, author, journal, and number of pages in the article. Students can choose either HTML or PDF full text articles to be printed, saved, or e-mailed. Again, a brief scan of the abstract allows quick determination of the usefulness or appropriateness of the article or study for inclusion into the literature review.

It is important to note that while some databases are more focused on the sciences, others are more concentrated on the humanities. High school libraries often purchase usage licenses for several databases to offer their students a variety of reliable sources of information, whereas college and university libraries purchase subscriptions to dozens of databases that students should learn to access and use effectively. One need only access a college library's website to view a list of available databases. These databases are generally limited to use by the individual library's constituency. Utilizing databases effectively is a skill that should be developed by high school students and is a requisite skill for college-bound individuals and adults working in information-based positions and industries.

Workshop 3: Making It Meaningful: Browsing Databases/Finding Information

Learning Goals: The goal of this workshop is for the student to understand how databases are used to organize knowledge and the role of a database in information gathering for a scientific study.

Location: Computer Lab

Team: Teacher, Librarian, and Resource Guide

Inquiry Unit: This workshop shall provide the student the opportunity to familiarize or refamiliarize herself with the databases so that she can begin actively browsing available source information.

Total Time: 50 minutes

Starter Time: 15 minutes	The teaching team begins the introduction to or review of databases by asking the student if she knows what a database is and if the student can distinguish between a database and a search engine. The librarian will then describe what a database is, what it may hold, and what a search engine does. The research guide should be experienced using databases. The teaching team will get some sense of the student's experience with databases. The team will also distinguish between different kinds of databases: science, the humanities, subject specific, general information, and so on.
Work Time Time: 25 minutes	Students refer to their brainstorming sheets. Before jumping into the electronic databases and especially for those students who have no topic ideas, the teaching team will provide a small collection of current print magazines such as *Scientific American*, *Psychology Today*, *Wired*, and *The New York Times'* *Science Times*. Other print materials will include specialized encyclopedias on psychology, health, disease and disorders, sports, and environment. Students will be asked to browse through the print materials and brainstorm topical ideas for search terms. Students are then asked to search for a general press (GP) article in one of the two or three suggested databases. The teaching team will monitor and assist with searching. If the student finds an article of interest she will ask one of the teaching teams if it is suitable to be printed. Upon approval, the article should be printed.
Reflection Time: 10 minutes	Students can discuss the difficulty or ease of database searching. They can also discuss how to find a meaningful topic using search terms. The students will discuss how the chosen topic works for the student and whether it fits the assignment. Finally, students can discuss how a GP article provides more information to formulate other scientific search terms.
Notes	Your students may already be comfortable and experienced using databases. You may combine needed elements of this workshop with **Workshop 5: Researching the Introduction**. However, preserve some browsing time so that each student may explore the feasibility and interest level of her topic, and find one or more GP article(s).

Common Core Standards	CCSS.ELA-Literacy.RI.11-12.7: Integrate and evaluate multiple sources of information presented in different media or formats (e.g., visually, quantitatively), as well as in words in order to address a question or solve a problem. CCSS.ELA-Literacy.W.11-12.7: Conduct short as well as more sustained research projects toanswer a question (including a self-generated question) or solve a problem; narrow or broaden the inquiry when appropriate; synthesize multiple sources on the subject, demonstrating understanding of the subject under investigation. CCSS.ELA-Literacy.W.11-12.8: Gather relevant information from multiple authoritative print and digital sources, using advanced searches effectively; assess the strengths and limitations of each source in terms of the task, purpose, and audience; integrate information into the text selectively to maintain the flow of ideas, avoiding plagiarism and overreliance on any one source and following a standard format for citation.

Handout #1: Databases for the Scientific Literature Review

A database is an electronically held collection of newspapers, magazines, transcripts, and scholarly journals. Imagine a library in cyberspace that is full of years of articles from these sources. That is a database. Some databases are larger than others. Some contain only scientific articles, while others contain only humanities articles. Some databases contain general information, while others are very specific. There is no all-inclusive or perfect database—some databases share materials, while other databases have exclusive access to materials. Many university libraries have subscriptions to dozens of different databases. If you access a university library's website, you can probably view its list of subscription databases, but you will not be able to access the articles.

The following is a list of the databases this library subscribes to that may assist you in your research. The librarians want to make sure you know how to access them. It is possible that you will need usernames and passwords to access the databases—the library has a list of them. If you need assistance, please ask! Be aware that home access depends upon the school library's licensing agreement.

1. *eLibrary*: Good for background and general information, but also includes peer-reviewed or scholarly journals.

   Internet address: _____
   Username: _____
   Password: _____
   Access from home: Y   [ ] or N   [ ]

2. *ProQuest*: An excellent source for scholarly/peer-reviewed journal studies.

   Internet address: _____
   Username: _____
   Password: _____
   Access from home: Y   [ ] or N   [ ]

3. *EBSCOhost*: A family of databases that can be searched separately or together. After entering EBSCO host, click on EBSCOhost web and check the desired databases. The databases most helpful for this project are Marshall Cavendish Reference Center (for general information), MasterFILEPremier, and Psychology & Behavioral Sciences Collection (for scholarly/peer-reviewed journal articles).

   Internet address: _____
   Username: _____
   Password: _____
   Access from home: Y   [ ] or N   [ ]

An example of a peer-reviewed journal that you might find in print copy on the library shelves or in an electronic database is:

Nature Magazine: Both *ProQuest* and *EBSCO* provide only abstracts for the previous 12 months, but the library has back issues for full text. Full text, with some exceptions, is available for older issues in both *ProQuest* and *EBSCO*. Please take a look at the hard copy (paper print) edition to familiarize yourself with this format of peer-reviewed journal.

Sample Database handout was created by Claudia Hesler (2010).

From *Teaching the Scientific Literature Review: Collaborative Lessons for Guided Inquiry*, by Randell K. Schmidt, Maureen M. Smyth, and Virginia K. Kowalski. Santa Barbara, CA: Libraries Unlimited. Copyright © 2014.

Handout #2: Search Glossary and General Tips

Definitions

- *Query*: An information request; a question in a form that a database or search engine can understand (this is different for various databases or search engines).
- *Browsing for Information*: To look for information casually, briefly scanning; "surfing," or shopping.
- *Database (DB)*: Data that are organized in an electronic file to enable searching and retrieval.
- *Search Engine*: A software program that retrieves information from a database and ranks its relevance to the searcher's query. Different search engines rank differently; Google, for example, is a search engine.
- *Search Keyword*: Search of words in the database fields, such as title, author, and abstract.
- *Search Subject*: A search of assigned subject headings in the database—the exact word(s) or phrase(s).

Boolean Operators

- AND: Commands the database to search and retrieve results with *all* the words.
- OR: Commands the database to retrieve results containing *any* and *all* keywords.
- NOT: Commands the database to retrieve results containing one keyword and not the other.

Use Good Search Strategies

- Use suggested terms.
- Use phrases where appropriate (e.g., vitamin A).
- Use truncation or wildcards where appropriate (child* to get child and children and childhood).

Finding Too Much?

- Use Booleans (i.e., depression AND women; diabetes AND children; coronary OR heart).
- Get more specific in word choice (nightmare instead of dreams).
- In advanced searches, target a field (such as subject) and use limiters (select peer reviewed, select date range or narrow it).

Finding Too Little?

- Check your query (spelling, date range).
- Query may be too long or complicated (depression and women and elderly and diet and vegetarian).
- Use broader terms.

Finding Nothing?

- Check spelling
- Query may be too narrow
- Confirm correct database
- Try new search terms (check synonyms, etc.)

From *Teaching the Scientific Literature Review: Collaborative Lessons for Guided Inquiry*, by Randell K. Schmidt, Maureen M. Smyth, and Virginia K. Kowalski. Santa Barbara, CA: Libraries Unlimited. Copyright © 2014.

Handout #3: Keeping Track
of Information Search

Record all relevant source details as you search. Why? You must document your sources, to retrieve sources again, and to refine your topic and/or search strategies. You may duplicate this form as you work with more sources.

1. Database: _____ Date Accessed: _____

   Search Terms Used: _____

   Article Title: _____

   Source Title (magazine, etc): _____

   Author(s): _____

   URL Address/DOINumber: _____

2. To use EasyBib: See Handout 1: Using EasyBib to Start the Reference List in **Workshop 6: Starting the Reference List.**

3. Instructions on notes to put on first page of each general press and peer-reviewed article:

   You will print out each general press article used for your introduction and every peer-reviewed study or white paper used for your Results of Research. You must note on the top of the first page of the printout whether it is a general press article by writing "GP." If it is a peer-reviewed study or white paper, write "PR." Add "white paper" to indicate that it is not a study. You must also note the search terms used to find the article or study in quotes. Highlight or note the date you accessed the study. Finally, highlight the title of the article or study, the author(s), the source of publication, the date of publication, and the Digital Object Identifier (DOI) number, if available.

Workshop 4

Creating and Organizing the Research Folder

Overview

Creating and organizing the research folder are essential to the scientific literature review (SLR) unit. Teachers can tell the student that the research folder is his learning portfolio. By conducting this SLR, each student is evolving into the role of researcher/scientist. An essential element is that the student approaches his research folder in an orderly fashion to allow for accountability and replication of the research. A carefully planned folder takes the place of a notebook and provides the student and teacher with easy reference. While the student is able to conveniently track assignments and access collected articles, teachers can periodically check the student's folder to make sure all articles are current and that the required number of general press (GP) articles and peer-reviewed (PR) studies are included in the folder. Annotations and student summaries of the readings can also be checked.

The research process can be likened to a journey a traveler is about to take and the folder can be analogous to a suitcase. As the traveler/researcher accumulates more input, information, and artifacts about the journey, the contents of the suitcase/folder accumulate and become defined. For the purposes of the SLR, a heavy gauge, durable 8 1/2 × 11" folder with two pockets will do nicely. Teachers can attach a label to the front of each folder and tell each student that he must print his name on the folder before including anything in the folder itself. The student is required to bring his folder with him to every workshop. Any handouts, hard copies of articles, electronic printouts of GP articles, scientific studies, and all drafts of the SLR must be kept in this folder. The folder represents the student's journey from novice researcher to scholarly scientist.

We recommend that the folder be specifically organized with all handouts received in chronological order in the left pocket. All research materials collected for the SLR can be maintained in the *right* pocket. This includes copies of introductory information gathered from GP articles and scholarly scientific studies found in database searches. All annotations are directly placed on the printouts of the articles.

Introductory material is found in sources that the general public might encounter, such as newspapers, magazines, documentaries, radio text, and so on. These sources are labeled general press or GP and are distinguished from the more distinct scholarly scientific studies. GP information is used only in the introduction to the SLR, *never* in the body of the SLR.

GP information serves the purpose of telling the student researcher what the world at large is saying about the topic being examined. When a student researcher encounters several sources of GP information about his research topic, he will probably get a broader perspective about what is popularly known regarding his topic. He will also build a better search vocabulary to use when researching the databases to find scholarly scientific studies reporting about aspects of his topic that are being researched.

The student should be reminded that GP articles report what the *world* is saying about a topic, whereas scientific studies report what *scientists* are researching and saying about the topic. Therefore, the GP article may only be used for the introduction to the SLR and the scholarly studies for the body of the SLR.

All scientific studies obtained from databases will include an Introduction, a Methodology (or Procedures), Results of Research, Analysis of the Research, Conclusion, and References, and should be clearly marked with PR for peer-reviewed scientific studies. Each article and each study included in the right pocket should contain a student-generated paraphrased summary of the study or article on the back of the printout. The summary of the article/study is explained in **Workshop 7: How to Read and Take Notes from a General Press Article** and **Workshop 10: How to Read and Take Notes from a Peer-Reviewed Journal Study or White Paper**. The student's job is easier when it comes to actually writing the literature review if all the GP articles and PR studies have been summarized immediately after the student has read them and then placed them in the folder. An organized folder enables the student to be responsible for the source materials that he will eventually use to produce the text, citations, and a reference list. The student is taught organizational skills and responsibility for the information collected and cited, skills that can be used again and again in other research projects and in college. When the student maintains an organized folder, he also assists the teacher in tracking the student's progress. The teacher can suggest additional resources the student might use to fill out the report and, if needed, verify a student's citations. (See Handout 1 in **Workshop 18: Putting It All Together to Hand Over the Scientific Literature Review to the Teacher** for a checklist of the completed research folder.)

Workshop 4: Creating and Organizing the Research Folder

Learning Goals: The goal of this workshop is for the student to understand what information must be collected and how to organize the information into the research folder.

Location: Library

Team: Teacher, Librarian, and Resource Guide

Inquiry Unit: This workshop will answer the following questions: How can the student organize his information to more easily use it? How do organizational skills relate to the assignment's expectations such as plagiarism, meeting assignment requirements, and quality results?

Total Time: 50 minutes

Starter Time: 10 minutes	The teacher will pass out the research folder to each student and have him write his name on the front label if that has not yet been done. The teacher explains what should be placed in the right and left pockets of the folder. See Handout 1 in **Workshop 18: Putting It All Together to Hand Over the Scientific Literature Review to the Teacher** for an organizational checklist. The librarian will hand out copies of the *Publication Manual of the American Psychological Association* (APA style guide) and point out within the manual the kinds of information necessary for a complete citation in the references (authors, article title, book or journal name, date, etc.). All the citation information must be highlighted on the student's print outs as it will be useful in citations and preparations of the methodology and reference list.
Work Time Time: 30 minutes	Students place in their folders whatever materials they have already printed, being sure to highlight all the citation information. Students may use Handout 1 and Handout 2 in **Workshop 18: Putting It All Together to Hand Over the Scientific Literature Review to the Teacher** for starting to organize the research folder. Students highlight all citation material in any print outs or printed information being placed in the folder. The librarian points out that all utilized materials must be included in the research folder before the instructor will correct the complete draft paper. This not only allows for a review of how the student used the ideas presented in the resources, but also how the student gave credit to the authors of those ideas. The librarian tells the student to review the school plagiarism policy available on the school website and/or in the student handout.
Reflection Time: 10 minutes	Students can discuss how they will keep their research organized in the research folder and why it must be organized. Students can also discuss how organizational skills relate to assignment deadlines, plagiarism, assignment requirements, the quality of results, and understand the severity of plagiarism.
Notes	• Remaining workshop time, approximately 10 minutes, can be used for more browsing. • Smart boards may be used to display APA information and Handout 1 and Handout 2 in Workshop 18 to begin organizing the research folder. • Instructors may choose to have students use a binder or an electronic research portfolio instead of a research folder.

From *Teaching the Scientific Literature Review: Collaborative Lessons for Guided Inquiry*, by Randell K. Schmidt, Maureen M. Smyth, and Virginia K. Kowalski. Santa Barbara, CA: Libraries Unlimited. Copyright © 2014.

Common Core Standards	*CCSS.ELA-Literacy.W.11-12.8*: Gather relevant information from multiple authoritative print and digital sources, using advanced searches effectively; assess the strengths and limitations of each source in terms of the task, purpose, and audience; integrate information into the text selectively to maintain the flow of ideas, avoiding plagiarism and overreliance on any one source and following a standard format for citation.

Research in the Selection Stage of the Information Search Process

Workshop 5: Researching the Introduction
Workshop 6: Starting the Reference List
Workshop 7: How to Read and Take Notes from a General Press Article
Workshop 8: How to Write the Introduction

During the Selection Stage, four workshops are scheduled and detailed herein. This is the time when students choose, read, and note the introductory material about a scientific question they are examining. The introductory material is general press information, which will later assist the student in searching for scientific studies about the chosen topic. Unstructured time also should be scheduled for students to search, read, and summarize their introductory articles and finish the composition of the Introduction. Librarians should be available to assist students who may not find enough different sources or who get stuck in the search. During selection, students will display optimism as a topic comes into view and the research project is personalized.

Workshop 5

Researching the Introduction

Overview

By now, the student has had several workshops that have established the process for undertaking a scientific literature review (SLR), the format required, the organizational skills necessary to keep the research folder arranged so it can be a helpful tool for both the student and teacher, and a cursory introduction to (or refresher on) databases and browsing for information. During this period, the student may actively examine topics she finds to be of interest. It is common for a student to be interested in pursuing topics for which she might have a personal connection. For some students, the topic might be centered on an inquiry that satisfies a personal or family issue. Perhaps, there is a son with a history of diabetes in his family or a daughter trying to understand the treatment of her mother who was recently diagnosed with breast cancer. Or it might be a student who was just introduced to String Theory in physics class and now wants to examine more thoroughly the scientific principles involved. Whether the student comes to the SLR with some preconceived thoughts or needs an opportunity to browse for information to formulate a question, it is now time for the student to be introduced to the general press (GP) literature.

To complete the introduction section, the student will need at least six GP articles that must be less than five years old. These articles will provide the student with an introduction to what the world at large is saying about a chosen topic. Most libraries keep copies of newspapers of note (such as *The New York Times*, in which editors and journalists have a solid background of the sciences), subscription magazines (from reputable publishers that discuss a variety of topics), or specialized encyclopedias or books (either in print or electronic format) on scientific subjects; any of these sources would be a good place to start. The librarian might offer the student a handout with an overview of possible print and electronic media sources to help with some avenues of initial research. Suggesting that the student use at least two or three different types of resources presents her with possible introductory material, varying points of view, and an informed vocabulary that focuses future searches. If a student locates an article that she decides to incorporate into her Introduction, she should copy that article as well as the publication information and place the copy in the right-hand pocket of the research folder. Remind the student to ask questions to the instructors, who can steer her to possible resources.

After the student has explored materials in the library, she will have a more informed view of the topic as well as a working vocabulary to find other materials. Now, the student will need to expand her exploration and knowledge by extending search efforts to include the library's electronic databases. Before beginning the database search, remind her to keep track of the search terms she is using, as she is required to list those search terms in the methodology section of the paper she produces. One easy way to list the search terms which the student uses is by writing the search term in quotation marks at the top of the printout of the GP article she uses. This eliminates any repetition, allows for a greater variety of articles being retrieved, and is an essential requirement for preparing the Methodology section of the SLR. It is best if the librarian or teacher shows the student how to do a sample search and provides her with a list of available databases (see Workshop 3, Handout 1). After this demonstration, the student should take a turn searching for articles on her own. She should be well-equipped with a working formal vocabulary to help find appropriate articles, and at the same time should be discouraged from using any slang while searching. Whether using databases such as *eLibrary*, which focuses on more generalized articles, or *ProQuest*, which also contains large newspaper holdings, remind the student to search several available databases in order to adequately cover her topic.

To begin a search, the student can use the basic search mode on the database, which is relatively easy, by entering a search term or terms. The student then sets the date range to within a five-year period, indicates full text articles, and performs the search. A preliminary review of the returned menu of articles listing title, author, source, and date of publication might provide evidence as to whether an article should be selected or discarded. At this point, the student can determine if the potential article is relevant or enough to read. The decision to read or not read can only be made by the student, who should be thinking about her topic as she chooses articles. *Only what may seem meaningful to the student should be read.* If the article is selected, the student should begin by carefully reading the abstract before making a final determination to print the whole article. Any printed articles that meet the criteria for inclusion into the introduction should be marked GP for general press article and placed in the right-hand pocket of the research folder. As the student selects and prints the GP articles, she may begin to compose a list of references for her SLR reference list. The next **Workshop 6: Starting the Reference List** will begin the task of creating a reference list.

Workshop 5: Researching the Introduction

Learning Goals: The goal of this workshop is for the student to begin collecting GP source material for the construction of the introduction.

Location: Library

Team: Teacher, Librarian, and Resource Guide

Inquiry Unit: This workshop shall provide the answers to the questions: What is information authority? How does the general press reflect/report science knowledge? Is there more than one type of information? Is there enough general press information on my topic?

Total Time: 50 minutes

Starter Time: 15 minutes	The teaching team will display examples of an array of general press (GP) articles addressing one or more topics. Using the student's previously approved GP article, the teaching team will distinguish between GP sources and peer-reviewed sources to ensure that students utilizing databases do not jump to detailed scholarly works during the preliminary searches for introductory materials. The teaching team will also review the need for updated five-year-old or newer sources of full text information. Only what is meaningful to the student should be read and used by the student. If the article is of interest, the student should then begin by carefully reading the abstract before making a final determination to print out the whole article.
Work Time Time: 25 minutes	Students are asked to reread the approved GP article printed during the previous class. Students who have a vague idea or have formulated an inarticulate question can begin with a database search, using the language of the approved article. The student constructs a search query using general subject terms or synonyms. For those students without a topic, the teaching team can distribute print magazines and newspapers. For example, some sources to use are *The New York Times* (a *Science Times* article is especially good), a significant article of a major newspaper, a chapter of a book (fiction or nonfiction) about the student's particular subject, and an article from a current magazine (a reputable publisher required) that discusses some aspect of the student's topic. Other sources are listed on the student handout. The student should locate two additional articles or other items on her topic from GP sources, and then determine if and how a search query must be adjusted. The teaching team should continue to monitor searches and initial approved printouts. Students should be reminded to use GP sources verified by the teaching team, not scholarly work. Those students who are struggling to solidify a topic idea may brainstorm with the teaching team and be further guided. Students should be reminded to keep a running reference list of their source information throughout the entire research process. The next workshop, **Workshop 6: Starting the Reference List**, will guide the student toward starting the Reference List.

From *Teaching the Scientific Literature Review: Collaborative Lessons for Guided Inquiry*, by Randell K. Schmidt, Maureen M. Smyth, and Virginia K. Kowalski. Santa Barbara, CA: Libraries Unlimited. Copyright © 2014.

Reflection Time: 10 minutes	Students can discuss among themselves a possible research topic from their approved digital and print source material. Students will discuss how much information is enough to complete their introduction. Finally, students can discuss where and how they can find the best information sources to fit their needs, how much science they have encountered in the GP articles, and what were the limitations of the articles.
Notes	• If there are not enough computers for students to search electronic databases individually, students can work in pairs or teams helping one another or print materials can be used. A smart board can be used to display examples of GP articles in the print or digital version. • The number of GP sources required for this assignment may be fine-tuned to reflect circumstances and demands, including available time for project, student abilities, librarian and/or teacher availability for instruction and assessment, and intended final paper length.
Common Core Standards	*CCSS.ELA-Literacy.W.11-12.8*: Gather relevant information from multiple authoritative print and digital sources, using advanced searches effectively; assess the strengths and limitations of each source in terms of the task, purpose, and audience; integrate information into the text selectively to maintain the flow of ideas, avoiding plagiarism and overreliance on any one source and following a standard format for citation. *CCSS.ELA-Literacy.RST.11-12.5*: Analyze how the text structures information or ideas into categories or hierarchies, demonstrating understanding of the information or ideas.

Handout: Researching the Introduction to Your Scientific Literature Review

As you are aware, you need six or more GP articles for the Introduction of your SLR. You must access, read, annotate, and incorporate these sources into the Introduction of your SLR. To help you gather these GP sources, we offer you a list below from which you may pick and choose at least two or three different types. (*Please note*: Sources must be less than *five years old*, unless you are using a classic text such as Rachel Carson's *Silent Spring* on pesticides.)

Some Sources You Might Use

1. *The New York Times* (a *Science Times* article is especially good)
2. Significant article of a major newspaper
3. Chapter of a book (fiction or nonfiction) about your particular subject
4. Article from a current magazine (a reputable publisher required) that discusses some aspect of your topic
5. Poem
6. Performance or play
7. Work of art
8. Interview on *National Public Radio* (NPR) or other similar source (text version is helpful)
9. Television program on your topic
10. Photograph or exhibition
11. Documentary
12. Website page or article (from reputable information source such as CNN); should be teacher approved
13. Specialized (not general) encyclopedia (e.g., *Encyclopedia of the Vietnam War* for an article on Agent Orange)
14. Reputable podcast; should be teacher approved
15. Other sources will be considered

From *Teaching the Scientific Literature Review: Collaborative Lessons for Guided Inquiry,* by Randell K. Schmidt, Maureen M. Smyth, and Virginia K. Kowalski. Santa Barbara, CA: Libraries Unlimited. Copyright © 2014.

Workshop 6

Starting the Reference List

Overview

Scientific writing must be carefully cited and documented for intellectual property rights and scholarly continuity, so that other scientists can verify existing scientific procedures and findings. The student writing a Reference List is preparing an information pathway. In preparing a scientific literature review (SLR), the student should adhere to the recommendations set forth in the American Psychological Association (APA) style manual or other approved, acknowledged, scientific style manuals. APA style is a standard adopted for reporting information in the scientific arena and is required for this project in documenting citations within the text for all scientific literature, as well as by documenting reference sources in the Reference List. If the teacher prefers a different style manual, then the student should utilize the same manual preferred by the teacher. Several copies of the latest edition of the *Publication Manual of the American Psychological Association* or other chosen science style manual should be available for the student to use in and out of the classroom. APA style information can also be found online. In addition, the student should refer to Handout 2 for this section, which provides an example of a student-generated Reference List written in APA style.

Unlike the Modern Language Association (MLA) style, which is used extensively in humanities research and in which citations appear at the end of the sentence or passage, citations for the APA style are placed within the text of the sentence. The citation is generally placed after the first or main subject term of the borrowed or referenced information, usually at the beginning of the sentence. Citations are indicated by parentheses and include the author's last name followed by a comma and the year of publication of the article. Variations such as multiple authors, works by anonymous authors, works with no author given, or direct quotations should be checked against the APA style manual for appropriate citations.

When preparing the Reference List, the student should check to make sure that all the citations included in the text of the SLR are accounted for in the Reference List. The student should use all articles and studies or white papers inserted into his folder and check these against his citations; any information borrowed from articles and studies and placed in the student's text *must* be cited. Once this has been accomplished, the student can begin to arrange the sources used in alphabetical order by the first author's last name. References are written in alphabetical order and double spaced, with the second and third line (if needed) of the entry indented. Please refer students to Handout 2. Information such as the author's name, year of the article, title, publication, volume, and pages are included in the Reference List, as is the database information and date the student accessed the article. Authors' names should appear in the Reference List in the order they appear in the article. In the case of multiple authors, the first author's last name should be indicated in the Reference List first, followed by the other names. There should be no attempt by students to rearrange the last names indicated, either in the text citation or in the Reference List. Journals, names of the newspapers, and titles of books should all be italicized. When no author is indicated, the article is included in the Reference List by the editor's name; if no editor is indicated, the title of that article goes first in the Reference List entry. Further variations will arise while a student is preparing the Reference List and these should be reconciled using the APA style manual. While the reference list will not be complete until later in the research process, the student has now begun to document his research.

For students with access to online bibliography creation services such as EasyBib, it is easier to compose a reference list using the APA style. EasyBib, for example, will be able to find the information necessary and format it into an APA style bibliographical entry, with the student providing basic information about the source. (See the student Handout 1.)

Workshop 6: Starting the Reference List

Learning Goals: The goal of this workshop is to introduce the student to a scientific standard of preparation of a reference list for the student's research of a SLR.

Location: Computer lab or Library

Team: Teacher, Librarian, and Resource Guide

Inquiry Unit: This workshop will provide the answers to the following questions: What role does the reference list play in scientific research? Why must researchers document information sources? Why follow a specific style of documentation? What references must be listed? And how should they be organized? What is a reference list generator on the web?

Total Time: 50 minutes

Starter Time: 15 minutes	The teaching team hands out and displays examples of a study's reference list. They use this example to introduce scholarly work and reinforce the difference between general press (GP) source information. Students will be introduced to APA style and works cited formatting. EasyBib is the recommended bibliography generator. Using the sample study's reference list, create a sample account and ask students to follow along and do the same. Input a variety of source types into the EasyBib generator together. Students will be instructed to initiate a digital account and be instructed on the manual and automatic input options. This is a good opportunity to remind students that while the reference list ultimately gives the reader an indication of the researcher's use of sources, it can also be used to advance the student's own research. Students should be encouraged to ride the citation wave using proper names, institutions, organizations, and so on found in the reference lists of articles and studies the student will acquire and information sources that the student will encounter.
Work Time Time: 25 minutes	Once each student has made an EasyBib account, he can spend class time inputting source information from the articles he has already collected. By now, students should have obtained three or four GP sources. The automatic citation option of EasyBib cannot always locate complete information, so the teaching team should supervise the creation of the student's EasyBib accounts and help students input source information to obtain the most accurate reference entry. After the student has created his account and inputted source information, he can seek another article on a database with similar source information for his paper.
Reflection Time: 10 minutes	Students will discuss as a group whatever problems they had setting up their electronic EasyBib accounts for the reference list and the relationship of the reference list to creating a trail of the student's accountability for his research.
Notes	The librarian and science teacher may allow the student to utilize an online reference list generator. EasyBib is just one such generator. Online services (fee based or free) can produce excellent results, although not every time. The student must fully understand the various components that make up each reference entry. If students do not yet understand the components of a reference entry, the librarian can provide a tutorial and use the APA manual to provide a concrete example. In addition, adequate time should be spent teaching the correct in-text citation format.

From *Teaching the Scientific Literature Review: Collaborative Lessons for Guided Inquiry*, by Randell K. Schmidt, Maureen M. Smyth, and Virginia K. Kowalski. Santa Barbara, CA: Libraries Unlimited. Copyright © 2014.

Common Core Standards	CCSS.ELA-Literacy.W.11-12.8: Gather relevant information from multiple authoritative print and digital sources, using advanced searches effectively; assess the strengths and limitations of each source in terms of the task, purpose, and audience; integrate information into the text selectively to maintain the flow of ideas, avoiding plagiarism and overreliance on any one source and following a standard format for citation.
	CCSS.ELA-Literacy.RST.11-12.5: Analyze how the text structures information or ideas into categories or hierarchies, demonstrating understanding of the information or ideas.

Handout #1: Using EasyBib to Start the Reference List

EasyBib is a citation tool for creating Reference Lists (used in APA and Chicago styles) and Works Cited (used in MLA style). It supports MLA, APA, and Chicago/Turabian styles. For most sources, EasyBib will be able to create the information needed for the bibliographic entry. If not, a fill-in-the-blank form will allow you to enter the necessary information. EasyBib will then correctly format it per the chosen style. *As always, it is your responsibility to double check that the entry is correct. Due to the nature of the internet, the instructions below are subject to change.*

Save your completed bibliography to a place accessible later. (*See 5 below*)

To use EasyBib:

From a computer connected to the school network go to http://easybib.com.

1. Follow the Login or Register prompt. Choose Register and fill in the form to create an account. This account information can now be used to access EasyBib from any computer with internet access.
2. Click Create New Project. Name the project, choose style, and click Create.
3. Under Project, choose Bibliography. Select type of entry: book, website, database, and so on.
4. You may use the autocite option by typing in the article or book title. (You should be aware that the automatic entry may not be the exact information needed for the reference list.) If EasyBib can find the articles or books matching the title, it will list them. Select the correct one. Double check that the format is correct: In Print, Online, or Online Database. Items that may be missing from the entry are outlined in red. Often, this includes the database name and date accessed. Click Create Citation.
5. After all the sources are entered, there are several options. The list will be sorted alphabetically regardless of the order entered. The list can be e-mailed or saved as a Word document or a Google document. The information will remain in EasyBib in the project created.
6. There is an option to cut and paste your bibliography into a Word document. DO NOT use this option. This will change the formatting of the document.

In general, EasyBib will format your reference list. But if changes need to be made, go back into EasyBib and replace the old list with the new changes. Remember to capitalize article or study titles, do not double space, *use the APA format,* and provide retrieval information, including a DOI, which identifies the document, and can be found in the PDF format of the document.

Sample Easybib handout was created by Claudia Hesler (2013).

Handout #2: Sample Reference List

Several online and print tools can be used to create an accurate *Reference List* or *Works Cited* page. You should title your *Works Cited* page(s) as a *Reference List* of those sources cited in the SLR. Your teacher may also request a list of all sources handled, not only those cited. As for the entire SLR, the APA style manual can be consulted for proper citation and formatting style.

In either case, the sources should be listed in alphabetical order using the last name of the first listed author of each study as the entry point. Multiple authors of a given study should be listed in the *exact* same name order as they are presented in the study. Below is a portion of a sample page of a student's references for a paper titled, "The Developmental, Cognitive, and Psychosocial Effects and Interference with Life Quality of Antiepileptic Treatments on Epilepsy Patients." The paper was written by Carl Brown in 2013.

Sample Reference List

Arana, A.M.D., Wentworth, C.E., M.S., Ayuso-Mateos, J.L., M.D., & Arellano, F.M., M.D. (2010). Suicide-related events in patients treated with antiepileptic drugs. *The New England Journal of Medicine*, 363, 542–551. Retrieved January 26, 2013, from www.proquest.com.

Caring for a child with Lennox-Gastout syndrome—It takes a village. (2012, November 8) *St. Joseph News*. Retrieved December 5, 2012, from www.proquest.com.

Cincinnati among sites for study of antiepileptic drugs in pregnancy. (2012, August 18) *US Fed News and Service*. Retrieved December 5, 2012, from www.proquest.com.

Devlin, H. (2009, August 4) Discovery of epilepsy gene is key to future treatment: Flaw may predispose half of sufferers to disease. *The Times*. Retrieved December 26, 2012, from www.proquest.com.

FDA requires warnings about risk of suicidal thoughts, behavior for antiepileptic medications. (2008, December 16). *US Fed News and Service*. Retrieved December 5, 2012, from www.proquest.com.

Gee, A. (2012, June 5) New epilepsy tactic: Fight inflammation. *New York Times*. Retrieved December 4, 2012, from www.proquest.com.

Assessment Rubric: Starting the Reference List

The Reference List is worth a maximum of 10 points toward the final grade.

10–9 points = Demonstrates excellent organization with all sources included in the proper APA format.

8–6 points = Demonstrates good organization with only minor omissions and/or errors in APA format.

5–0 points = Demonstrates poor organization with omission of sources and/or incorrect APA format.

Points are awarded for the following:

Criteria	Points Earned
Citations *(Worth 5 points)* • At least 12–16 sources are included	
Mechanics *(Worth 5 points)* Correct APA format is utilized Citations are to be: • Alphabetized • Indented (second line) • Listed by author in order indicated • Proper italicization and punctuation	
Total Points for the Reference List: *(Maximum 10 points)*	

Workshop 7

How to Read and Take Notes from a General Press Article

Overview

Once the student has found some of the six general press (GP) articles about the chosen topic, a lesson can be given on how to read and take notes from a GP article. The student should be reminded that the GP articles can be used only for the Introduction to the scientific literature review (SLR), and therefore the Introduction note-taking process differs from that of the scientific studies' note taking.

When taking notes for the Introduction, the student is searching for a broad sense of what the world is saying about the research topic. But, to depict this broad sense, the student must find several specific examples of what is being reported in the general press. In effect, each of the six GP articles becomes a specific example and contributes to a broad picture of what the world is saying about the research topic or question.

This is the time to get organized. The student needs to retrieve her GP articles, staple all the pages together for each article, and designate all articles on the first page of the printout as GP or general press. Teacher and student must check to make sure that the correct number of articles (six to eight) is accounted for. If a student is unsure that it is a GP article, she should clarify this with the teacher or librarian.

As the student approaches the first GP article, *she should use a highlighter, if she has not yet done so, to denote all citation information such as the author, title of article, source, and date.* (This will help the student later to prepare the Reference List.) The student should then begin to read the abstract of the article. If the student finds the abstract too difficult to understand or confusing, she should discard it and move on to another article. When the student finds an abstract that is understandable, she should proceed to read the whole article, briefly annotating and highlighting two types of information while reading. The student must find information that is interesting to her, as this is *her* SLR. She should look for and highlight an interesting or eye-catching statistic, statement, scenario, quote, or fact. After the student finds information to highlight that is interesting, she should make a one- to two-word annotation in the margin to help remind her why she chose to highlight this information.

Summarizing one article at a time while the information is still fresh in the student's mind is required. Having read and annotated the first article, the student should turn over the printout of the article and on the back write a direct quotation from the article using the startling information (statistic, quote, scenario, etc.). This direct quotation becomes an information hook! Once again, the student uses the back page of the article and proceeds to report on the information gleaned from the article in a one- to two-paragraph summary written in her own words. She uses the highlighted portions of the text and her annotations to remind her of the points to include in the summary. This process is repeated with each of the remaining five to seven articles. Each article collected and denoted GP should have a direct quotation and a one- to two-paragraph summary *in the student's own words* written directly on the back of that article. The summary should focus on the one or two most interesting or important aspects of the article to the student. Remind the student that she should not skimp on the summaries, but neither should she include any extraneous information: the student is reporting on what has been read and using the one or two words that she has placed in the margin of the article to help summarize the article in her own words.

After writing the summaries on the back of the printout, the student should reread her summaries and indicate underneath the summaries one or two words that remind her what the summary is about. She should then select what she considers the most interesting fact, figure, statement, scenario, or quote from among the six articles. Among the chosen quotations, the best choice from the six articles then becomes the hook for the Introduction. The student physically sorts the summaries by using the one- to two-word reminders to prioritize the articles. She should then number the summaries to present them in order, organizing them in a way that makes sense to the student and to the potential reader. The hook and the organized summaries become the student's text for her Introduction to the topic and the SLR. With the aid of citations for all borrowed materials (which is practically everything within the Introduction) and transitional phrases or sentences between sources, the introduction is written. The student can congratulate herself now as she has just completed approximately one-sixth of the SLR! At this point, librarians and teachers should identify those students who may need extra help.

Workshop 7: How to Read and Take Notes from a General Press Article

Learning Goals: The goal of this workshop is for the students to learn how to read and take notes from a GP article or piece of information from the popular media, to identify a hook, and compose a one- to two-paragraph summary of the borrowed information.

Location: Library or Classroom

Team: Teacher, Librarian, and Resource Guide

Inquiry Unit: This workshop will provide the answers to the following questions: What is interesting and important to me within the article I have found? How can I summarize the information that is most relevant and interesting?

Total Time: 50 minutes

Starter Time: 15 minutes	The teaching team will distribute the handout and ask each student to choose a short article about her chosen topic. They will ask the student to read her article. The student will use a highlighter and a pencil or pen to indicate the following: Author, publication title, date of publication, and database. The student will mark the article GP for general press. The student is then asked to read her own article and identify two types of information: 1. Information that the student thinks is interesting and relevant to her. 2. An eye catching statistic, statement, quote, fact, or scenario that highlights the topic. During the reading, after each piece of information is highlighted, the student should then immediately make a one- to two-word note next to the highlighting in the margin about why the material was highlighted.
Work Time Time: 25 minutes	After the article has been read, highlighted, and noted, the student should use the back of the article (and extra paper if needed) and proceed to report on the information gleaned from the article. To do so, the student will reread the highlighted material, look at her notes in the margin, and then turn the paper over and write a one- to two-paragraph summary in her own words about the article. Whatever startling statistic, statement, quote, fact, or scenario was highlighted should be quoted as well on the back of the page. At the end of the work time, students are informed that this process should be continued for each of the six GP sources. The teaching team will announce one or two more unstructured workshop dates to finish the work.
Reflection Time: 10 minutes	Students can discuss the purpose of communicating information from a GP source.

From *Teaching the Scientific Literature Review: Collaborative Lessons for Guided Inquiry*, by Randell K. Schmidt, Maureen M. Smyth, and Virginia K. Kowalski. Santa Barbara, CA: Libraries Unlimited. Copyright © 2014.

Notes	The number of GP sources required for this assignment may be fine-tuned to reflect numerous circumstances and demands, including available time for project, student abilities, librarian and/or teacher availability for instruction and assessment, intended final paper length, and so on. Sources may include films, documentaries, radio interviews, photographs, exhibitions, and so forth. The recommended length of the article summaries may be expressed in a range of paragraph numbers and/or word count. A summary of one to two paragraphs is the average target. Articles may vary in length or may contain overlapping information. The required length may also reflect the librarian and science teacher's assessments of student ability and be adjusted accordingly. The text of the summaries added together becomes the text of the introduction which should be approximately 1½ to 2 pages long.
Common Core Standards	*CCSS.ELA-Literacy.RI.11-12.7*: Integrate and evaluate multiple sources of information presented in different media or formats (e.g., visually, quantitatively), as well as in words in order to address a question or solve a problem. *CCSS.ELA-Literacy.RST.11-12.2*: Determine the central ideas or conclusions of a text; summarize complex concepts, processes, or information presented in a text by paraphrasing them in simpler but still accurate terms.

Handout: How to Read and Take Notes from a General Press Article

For this project, you need six or more GP articles for the *Introduction* of your SLR. To incorporate these sources into the *Introduction*, you must *read, highlight, annotate, and summarize* each article.

To Begin

1. Locate your research folder, a highlighter, and a pen or pencil
2. Locate a GP article

Steps for Taking Notes

1. Get organized: After first accessing it on a database, mark GP on the top of the printed article and the date it was printed. Make sure it is a GP article. Not sure? Ask! *Staple* pages together for each article reprint—paper clips can fall out.
2. Highlight the citation information (author, newspaper/source title, date, etc.).
3. Write the search term that you used to find the article in quotation marks on the top of the article.
4. Read the abstract and get a concise idea of what the article is about. Can you understand it? If not, it may not be the appropriate article for you and you should discard it.
5. If you understand the abstract, read the whole article.
6. Look for two things to highlight. By highlighting, you are choosing the information that is personally meaningful.

    a. Material that is surprising or interesting (fact, quotation, statistic, statement, or scenario).
    b. Information that is interesting or important to you—this is *your* literature review.

    Note on highlighting: do not be overzealous; try to highlight no more than 10–20 percent of the article!

7. Make brief annotations in the margin (1–2 words) to remind yourself what/why you highlighted. You will annotate again when you read the scientific studies.

Steps to Write the Summary

1. Turn over the article immediately after reading it and reviewing your brief annotations. You will now use the back page to write a summary in your own words. *By using the back page and not constantly rereading the text, you will avoid copying the text and plagiarizing. You will, instead, put the information in your own words.*
2. First, copy a direct quotation on the top of the page from the article. This is your startling or interesting fact, statement, statistic, or scenario—your hook to draw in your reader. Be sure to put quotation marks around it and indicate whose quotation it is.
3. Write a one- to two-paragraph summary of the article *in your own words*. This summary covers the information you found interesting in the GP article. Use the highlighted portions of the text and your one- or two-word annotations to remind yourself of the important information

The BIG Picture: HOW TO AVOID PLAGIARISM

- Why do this now? Because it is fresh in your mind!
- What do I do with this summary? This is the beginning of writing your *Introduction*. It will become the text of your *Introduction*. Except for your quote, your summary is in your own words.
- You will look at your six- to eight-article summaries. Find the best quotation (the "hook") from all the quotations you have chosen. Then, organize the summaries in a way that makes sense to you, so that you can present the information you found in the order you prefer.

From *Teaching the Scientific Literature Review: Collaborative Lessons for Guided Inquiry*, by Randell K. Schmidt, Maureen M. Smyth, and Virginia K. Kowalski. Santa Barbara, CA: Libraries Unlimited. Copyright © 2014.

- These grouped or organized summaries become the text for your *Introduction*. Connect them with transitional words, phrases, or sentences. Often, each summary will begin a new paragraph. *Each summary paragraph must have a citation of the source.*
- Do not skimp at this stage, but do not add either. *No fluff.* Give it your real consideration and focus on what the six articles say.

After summarizing all six articles, you will have about one-sixth of the paper done. How EASY is this?!?

We will continue to cover the Introduction in more detail in **Workshop 8: How to Write the Introduction.**

Workshop 8

How to Write the Introduction

Overview

The Introduction section of a scientific literature review (SLR) consists of information that the world at large is saying about the subject chosen by the student. It is comprised of information derived from general press (GP) articles from sources such as newspapers and magazines written by journalists about a scientific topic. There are *newspapers of note*, such as *The New York Times*, generally big city, reputable newspapers staffed by trained scientific writers and editors to review articles before allowing inclusion in the newspaper. Other popular press magazines such as *Popular Science, Astronomy*, and *Psychology Today* are not considered scientific journals but contain articles that are appropriate for inclusion in the Introduction section. Certain specialized, subject-related encyclopedias or reference works written by specialists in the sciences are also suitable for use.

When the student selects his first GP article for inclusion in the literature review and he reads and processes the information therein, he is actually developing a better understanding of the topic. GP articles tend to be written in nonscientific terminology or at least understandable scientific terminology, thus giving the student an introduction into what the world is saying about the chosen topic. The first two or three GP articles actually serve a dual purpose: allowing the student to develop a better understanding of the topic and providing a familiarity with the vocabulary used to explain the topic. This, in turn, allows the student to streamline his subsequent information search activities. His searches then become more purposeful, resulting in better keyword selection and more satisfactory results or hits. Each article collected and read builds a new broader knowledge of the topic, resulting in the student developing and pondering various questions that might arise in the research.

For the purpose of writing the Introduction to the SLR, each student should have collected six to eight GP articles. Before this, teachers and librarians, as guides, have been carrying the brunt of the responsibilities, explaining to each student what the project is all about, telling him how completing a SLR is beneficial, and teaching him how to manipulate and search databases. It is at this point when the student sits down to write the Introduction that he becomes more proactive. This is time for the educators to pass the torch of knowledge acquisition and critical thinking to the student, even though the student is reminded that the teacher will continue to help and guide him through the process. Now, the student undertakes his individual journey to become the expert, the researcher, and the scientist.

To help a student get ready to write his Introduction, the teacher should make sure that the student has indicated on the front of each article that it is a GP, or general press, article. (Marking the article with GP will assist the student in distinguishing that article from any peer-reviewed studies he collects later.) All GP articles should be printed out or copied; they must be read and a one- to two-paragraph summary of that article, in the student's own words, should be included on the back of the last page of the printout or copy.

It is important to tell the student at this point that he should focus solely on information that is interesting or important to him when annotating information from the chosen GP article, as this is the cornerstone to the guided-inquiry, student-centered research philosophy. This procedure, of annotating and then summarizing what is important to the student, should then be repeated with each of the remaining articles. Once the student has completed the annotations and summaries for all of the GP articles, he is ready to write.

Each GP article is represented by one to two paragraphs that summarize, *in the student's own words*, the topic discussed in the article. Each article summary will include an interesting or startling statistic, quote, statement, scenario, or fact which will be quoted. One of these will become the opening "hook" of the introduction. For example, a student writing about alcoholism might begin the Introduction with an article about genetics and alcohol use and might start by stating, "Scientists provide evidence that genetics . . ." (author, year, page number). The student should organize his summaries into whatever logical order he thinks makes the best sense. These summaries then become the text of the SLR Introduction when connected by words, transitional phrases, or sentences.

The seemingly daunting task of writing the Introduction to my Scientific Literature Review turned out to be significantly easier than I had first anticipated. After all, an Introduction provides the audience with their very first impression of what is to come, and I was initially unsure of how to go about making that the best impression possible.

However, I quickly learned that every step I had taken in preparing the general press articles I had found relating to my topic, would in turn allow me to cleanly piece together my Introduction without difficulty. Having already carefully reviewed and summarized each general press article, we were instructed to organize our summaries into groups pertaining to common subtopics of our main discussion. From there, there was left only the simple task of arranging each subtopic and summary in a logical order, essentially forming our Introduction.

This method made the process of writing my Introduction both uncomplicated and relatively quick in relation to what I had expected. Also, the lesson stressed the importance and benefits of careful reading and note taking early in the research process. These concepts were applicable to situations far beyond just the completion of this project. Indeed, the satisfaction of being able to incorporate my carefully written notes directly into my Introduction was enough to encourage further diligence as I continued along in the research and writing of my SLR. (Erin Mershon, student, Gill St. Bernard's School, 2007)

The student should be consistent in the placement of the citation for borrowed material. While there is no consensus of a single stylistic standard for where to place a citation for borrowed material within the text of a SLR, we recommend a simple rule for citation placement. Information that has been borrowed from another author or authors and has been either paraphrased or summarized and paraphrased should be cited in the following way: The citation, which includes the author's last name, a comma, and the year of publication and is held in parenthesis, should be placed immediately after the first subject term of the sentence(s) referring to or using the borrowed material. Unless the student stops using the borrowed material or begins using material from another source, the citation holds until the end of that paragraph. If the following paragraph continues to include the borrowed material, a new citation must be inserted after the first subject term of the new paragraph. This citation will hold through to the end of a new paragraph or until a new citation is added in the second paragraph. If a quotation of more than a few words is used, the American Psychological Association (APA) style manual demonstrates the formatting of the quotation and the citation placement.

For more information about citations, the student should be referred to the *Publication Manual of the American Psychological Association* (APA, 2010). *In this rule, because the Introduction and Results of Research sections contain only borrowed material, the student should have at least one citation at the beginning of each paragraph after the first subject term in the paragraph.*

Scientific writing can often be tedious to read even when written by the cleverest of scientists. One way to pique the reader's interest is for the student to develop a hook. Therefore, every student writing a SLR should write an Introduction that gets the reader interested—hooked—in the topic being explored. A hook allows a journey to begin; the student writer starts to contemplate and explore the possibilities while the reader is moved from complacency to curiosity.

So, just how does a student, who is a novice at writing a scientific review, get his audience hooked on what he has to say? One way to involve the reader might be to introduce an interesting statistic that the student discovered while reading the GP articles. A scenario that pits one scientific approach against another or describes a situation or issue might also be helpful. The student might also find in an article a definitive statement or fascinating quotation about the topic. So, if the student is researching DNA he might find a quotation that states, "The future of twenty-first-century medicine lies in what scientists are now discovering about genetics." The Introduction begins with this hook, which draws the audience/reader into the research and is followed by the summaries, each one cited, written in the student's own words, and organized by the student's own logic and choice for presentation. All borrowed material (which is almost everything in the Introduction) must be properly cited in the APA style.

Workshop 8: How to Write the Introduction

Learning Goals: The goal of this workshop is for the student to organize and arrange GP article summaries to write a research paper introduction.

Location: Library

Team: Teacher, Librarian, and Resource Guide

Inquiry Unit: This workshop will provide the answers to the following questions: How can I make sense of all the information I have located? What is the purpose of the introduction section of a science research paper? How do I use my GP summaries to organize and write my introduction?

Total Time: 50 minutes

Starter Time: 15 minutes	The goal of this workshop is for the student to understand, organize, and write his general press (GP) article summaries into a scientific research paper introduction. The teaching team will describe the purpose of an introduction section and distribute the handout. Using a student volunteer's summaries as an example, the teaching team will lead the class in organizing the summaries to prepare a model introduction.
Work Time Time: 25 minutes	Students will be asked to examine their six GP article summaries. They will identify the most powerful or attention-grabbing interesting fact, statement, scenario, or quote from among the six articles summaries to be used as the hook for the introduction. The students will then prioritize the summaries that they would like to present from first to last. With the teaching team's encouragement to utilize transition words and phrases, the students will then use the summaries to create a text as the introduction to the scientific literature review. The introduction should be approximately 1½–2 pages long. Each borrowed source should be cited with an in-text citation after the first subject term of each paragraph of borrowed information.
Reflection Time: 10 minutes	The student should read his *Introduction* to a partner. The partner should respond with questions and comments, and then the partner should read his introduction with the first student questioning and commenting.
Notes	The length of the introduction and number of sources may be increased or decreased according to individual student ability and/or class requirements, prerequisites, or level of difficulty. This workshop could be extended to two or three more class periods to ensure that all students complete the *Introduction*. Students will need table or floor space to spread out their articles and prioritize them for presentation in the *Introduction*.
Common Core Standards	CCSS.ELA-Literacy.W.11-12.2a: Introduce a topic; organize complex ideas, concepts, and information so that each new element builds on that which precedes it to create a unified whole; include formatting (e.g., headings), graphics (e.g., figures, tables), and multimedia when useful to aiding comprehension. CCSS.ELA-Literacy.RST.11-12.1: Cite specific textual evidence to support analysis of science and technical texts, attending to important distinctions the author makes and to any gaps or inconsistencies in the account.

From *Teaching the Scientific Literature Review: Collaborative Lessons for Guided Inquiry*, by Randell K. Schmidt, Maureen M. Smyth, and Virginia K. Kowalski. Santa Barbara, CA: Libraries Unlimited. Copyright © 2014.

Handout: How to Write the Introduction

Remember, you are merely reporting on what the world is saying (in the general press) about your subject.

I.   What is the function of the Introduction?

   A.   Get the reader interested

   B.   Give the reader some of the world's knowledge about your subject

   C.   Be sure the reader is informed of the scientific question or the guiding idea driving your research

II.   What to do with the six sources?

   A.   Get six sources of GP articles

   B.   Read them

   C.   Take notes

      1.   Underline

      2.   Highlight

      3.   Make brief side notes: 1–2 words

   D.   Find an interesting or startling fact, quotation, statement, statistic, or scenario. Put a * beside it to use for a possible "hook." Copy this quoted material on the back of the printout above your article summary. You may not end up using all the information.

   E.   Rereading your highlighted material and using your annotations, write a summary of one to two paragraphs in your own words on the back of your article printout.

   F.   Repeat for all six articles

   G.   Indicate in two words the main points in each article, after you have written the summary. Write those words in the same place on each summary.

   H.   Group the main points and organize them as you would like to present them by numbering the articles in a way YOU see fit, placing them first, second, third, and so on.

   I.   Start writing

      1.   Begin with the attention grabber—the hook. Use one of the six startling statistics, quotes, statements, scenarios, or facts.

      2.   Reread the organized points and summaries in the order they should be presented.

      3.   Transcribe the summaries, in your own words, as your basic paragraphs of text.

      4.   Be sure to use transitional sentences, phrases, or words to connect ideas as you write.

      5.   Be sure to cite the stuff you borrow from your sources in each paragraph.

      6.   Remember that you have borrowed almost everything for your Introduction and your Results sections.

III.   How long should it be?

   A.   The Introduction of your paper should be 1½–2 pages long.

   B.   Do not make things up. Stick to what the world is saying about your topic. Do not confuse what the world is saying with what you think.

   C.   We really do not want your opinion about the topic here. Stick to what you found in your GP research.

From *Teaching the Scientific Literature Review: Collaborative Lessons for Guided Inquiry*, by Randell K. Schmidt, Maureen M. Smyth, and Virginia K. Kowalski. Santa Barbara, CA: Libraries Unlimited. Copyright © 2014.

Assessment Rubric: Introduction

The Introduction is worth a maximum of 10 points toward the final grade.

10–9 points = Demonstrates excellent understanding through highly relevant source selection, an interesting hook, and well-organized information.

8–6 points = Demonstrates good understanding through relevant source selection, an interesting hook, and organized information.

5–0 points = Demonstrates incorrect or insufficient understanding through inconsistent or irrelevant source selection, an uninteresting hook, and poorly organized information.

Points are awarded for the following:

Criteria	Points Earned
Number of Citations (*Worth 5 points*) • Six to eight relevant general press (GP) articles included	
Research Subject Selection (*Worth 2 points*) • Scientific subject reflected in the content of all GP articles	
Hook (*Worth 2 points*) • States a relevant and interesting quotation, statistic, statement, scenario, or fact that engages the reader	
Mechanics and Grammar (*Worth 1 point*) • Correct spelling • Correct grammar • Correct APA format	
Total Points for the Introduction: (*Maximum 10 points*)	

Research in the Exploration Stage of the Information Search Process

Workshop 9: Searching for Peer-Reviewed Studies
Workshop 10: How to Read and Take Notes from a Peer-Reviewed Journal Study or White Paper

During the Exploration Stage, two workshops are conducted and detailed. During this stage, the student, in the structured workshop and in other unstructured work times, will be searching for, examining, noting, documenting and summarizing scientific studies or white papers that have been published in the last five years. These recent publications depict the study of some aspect of the student's research topic. At this stage, exploration of the research topic may be framed as a research question, although that question may not yet be fully articulated. The Teaching Team does not require the student's inquiry to be articulated as an actual research question. (See **Part 1, Chapter 2.**) Instead, the student is exploring an inarticulated question in which, lacking sufficient knowledge about the topic, she is making her way through complex materials that will help the researcher to explore and eventually examine enough information to articulate a research question.

Workshop 9

Searching for Peer-Reviewed Studies

Overview

The student has arrived at a critical point in the research process when peer-reviewed (PR) scientific studies must be searched for, reviewed, and chosen to be printed and read or discarded. She should be reminded that a PR journal study is a complete report of a scientific investigation and that the report is written so that others can learn about and from the study. This assignment calls for at least six studies to be reviewed. The search for pertinent PR studies begins as the student examines existing published studies, most of which are found in databases. She should be reminded that the six studies will present information that is less general and less broad than the general press (GP) articles. The studies will instead contain more specific, detailed, and scientific information.

At this point, the student can be reintroduced to the available databases and reminded that different databases hold different collections and provide access to specific journals. Some databases, for example, specialize in the biological or other sciences, and others, which are more general, may contain some scientific PR journals.

The format of the scientific literature review (SLR) is quite simple and almost universal in its application. The presentation of information in the literature review is the same as a presentation of an actual scientific study that is written. The presentation is also the same as a laboratory report of a scientific experiment. The literature review which the student will write contains the following seven sections:

1. *Cover Page and Abstract*
2. *Introduction*
3. *Methodology/Procedures (sometimes separated into participants, procedures and materials)*
4. *Results of Research*
5. *Analysis of Research*
6. *Conclusion*
7. *References*

The student should be shown a sample search on either a specialized or a general database, and then take a turn searching for a journal article that depicts a scientific study (not simply a journal article that depicts news, letters, a feature, or a book review). A journal study is a complete report of a scientific investigation depicting all the above-listed aspects of the investigation. The teacher should remind the student to cue the database search interface for a "peer reviewed" article that is shown with full text and to specify the five-year age span of the articles being called up. Only full text studies should be requested. Search terminology can be discussed and the student reminded to avoid slang or popular terms, and to search in favor of more formal or sophisticated topical terms found in GP articles and material already read and summarized. The student should be encouraged to use more than one term in the search for studies and to include scientists' names or scientific concepts found in the introductory literature while searching for studies.

Because the student needs experience in highly focused thinking, by searching for and quickly reviewing the article, reading the abstract (which is usually found just after the citation information at the top of the first screen interface holding the article content), and choosing to print and read or discard the particular articles, such focused thinking begins and critical research gets underway.

To ensure more successful research, the student should be allowed to browse through several articles in the initial search of PR studies. Eventually, the student will choose one study to print out while making annotations of search terms and databases that were successfully used. She might also be encouraged to use more than one database for experience in source and information differentiation. For the student who is unable to find at least two studies to print, assistance in searching should be offered. A tutorial in database usage is sometimes needed or a redirection of research focus may be necessary (see **Workshop 3: Making It Meaningful: Browsing Databases/Finding Information**).

The teacher and librarian may use the workshop to provide a list of accessible databases appropriate to the assignment and demonstrate useful search techniques. Expanding the search into the related search terms found in a given article, searching for an author or authors of similar studies, consulting the reference list of one study for possible other studies, and searching for conferences or research centers that focus on the topic are strategies that may provide more fruitful information pathways.

Finally, and most importantly, teachers must emphasize that there is *no perfect study*. In other words, the student will probably not find the study which precisely provides all the information the student may want. Each study is a small piece of a bigger picture comprising the research topic and no one study will completely answer the question driving the student's own research. But, if a study is readable and the student can understand the research question driving that study, then the student should continue to read. If she comprehends its Methodology and can make her way through the Results enough to understand some of the study and is able to follow some of the Analysis, then the study is useful, usable, and ready to be incorporated into the student's SLR.

All students, even the most enthusiastic, should be warned that an excessively long study is not the best option for this introductory literature review. A better choice would most likely be the 5- to-15-page studies. Quantity does not equal quality in scientific writing. One need only remember Einstein's $E = mc^2$!

As the student searches for studies and reads the abstracts, contradictory or oppositional positions or findings may be discovered. Encourage the student to pursue different voices and perspectives in the scientific literature. Encourage the student to consider the implications of studies that do not provide the expected results. She is looking for what is being reviewed, what has been found in the research, and what is being said in the literature, not simply one position therein. In fact, findings of similarly designed studies may and, in some cases, should differ. Different findings are part of the dynamics of scientific research. The student in her analysis will then examine such differences and why the differences occurred.

The search for PR studies may take several hours over several days and should not be rushed. A good search yields more material for a better paper. **Workshop 10: How To Read and Take Notes from a Peer-Reviewed Journal Study or White Paper** will teach the student how to read and handle PR studies.

Searching for a peer reviewed article proved to be the most important step in writing a scientific literature review. After reading over various general press articles on your topic, you begin to understand your topic in a general sense. Peer review studies allow the researcher to gain a deeper understanding of the subject. Using various databases is key to gaining articles that will give me, the researcher, interpretations from many different angles.

It is key to understand how to run a search on these databases. Once one becomes "search savvy" it is significantly easier to find articles that will contribute to the review. During the search process, it is easy to stay attached to one database, but it is essential to use as many different resources as possible. This gives the researcher many articles from various places, that provides the paper with scientific diversity.

After the peer reviewed articles are perused and summarized, the researcher gains key knowledge for the success of his/her literature review. It is important for researchers to use articles that can be interpreted by them because many peer reviewed articles are loaded with incomprehensible scientific lingo. The level of knowledge that is gained from this step brings the topic to the next level. Researchers find themselves writing like scientists and ultimately creating a paper that seemed to be an impossible task in the beginning, but has now been successfully developed. (Sean Johnson, student, Gill St. Bernard's School, 2007).

Workshop 9: Searching for Peer-Reviewed Studies

Learning Goals: The goal of this workshop is for the student to recognize a PR study, then search for and locate an appropriate study for the research paper.

Location: Library or Computer Lab

Team: Teacher, Librarian, and Resource Guide

Inquiry Unit: This workshop will provide the answers to the following questions: What does a PR study look like? What databases provide PR studies and how are they found? How should a search query be formulated? And can I find two PR studies?

Total Time: 50 minutes

Starter Time: 15 minutes	The goal of this workshop is to produce two peer-reviewed (PR) studies printed from databases containing scientific information. The teaching team will begin the workshop by passing around several copies of contemporary PR scientific studies. If a smart board or projector is available, the teaching team will project a study and point out how one is organized, where it was found, and what the student should be looking for when she begins her search. Students at this point should be encouraged to ask questions as the librarian is describing the organization of a study and how it can be found in a database. The teaching team will encourage the students to expand their searches by riding the citation wave of studies they find, searching related terms, and browsing extensively before printing. Highly focused thinking by reading the abstract is encouraged for the student to consciously choose or discard articles.
Work Time Time: 25 minutes	The students will be asked to formulate a simple search for a PR journal study. The query will be made up of search term(s) which the student has encountered during the introductory research of the general press articles. The student will be asked to find two PR studies about her research topic which should be examined and initialed by a member of the teaching team.
Reflection Time: 10 minutes	The class should come together to discuss the nature of a PR study. What does it look like? How do scientists communicate with each other and the general public? Has anyone found the perfect study? Is there such a thing as a perfect study? Is one study going to answer all the questions the student wants to answer?
Notes	The number of PR sources required for this assignment may be fine-tuned to reflect circumstances and demands, including available time for project, student abilities, librarian and/or teacher availability for instruction and assessment, intended final paper length, and so on. Note: If there are not enough computers for all students to search on the Internet, students can work in pairs or teams on a computer to help each other search. Other unstructured workshop times should allow for searching for PR studies, especially following **Workshop 10: How to Read and Take Notes from a Peer-Reviewed Journal Study or White Paper**.

Common Core Standards	CCSS.ELA-Literacy.W.11-12.8: Gather relevant information from multiple authoritative print and digital sources, using advanced searches effectively; assess the strengths and limitations of each source in terms of the task, purpose, and audience; integrate information into the text selectively to maintain the flow of ideas, avoiding plagiarism and overreliance on any one source and following a standard format for citation. CCSS.ELA-Literacy.RST.11-12.9: Synthesize information from a range of sources (e.g., texts, experiments, simulations) into a coherent understanding of a process, phenomenon, or concept, resolving conflicting information when possible.

Handout: Searching for Peer-Reviewed Studies

As you begin, remember the format of a scientific study: *Abstract, Introduction, Methods, Results, Analysis,* and *Conclusion.* It is similar to a lab report.

Search strategies for a peer-reviewed studies search:

- Use the databases suggested terms and any clusters/similar subjects/narrowing tools. Speak *the database's* language!
- Ride a citation wave: Use proper names/institutions/organizations from GP or other PR articles.
- Use a search phrase, instead of a single word, where appropriate (e.g., vitamin A).
- Select full text for the whole article view and printout.

Finding too much?

- **Is this a real study with all seven sections?**
- Narrow or refine search term with Booleans (e.g., depression AND women; diabetes AND children).
- Be more specific in word choice (nightmares instead of dreams).
- Use advanced search terms learned from your previous searching and introductory reading (myocardial infarction rather than heart attack).
- In advanced searches, use limiters (select peer-reviewed, select date range or narrow date range).

Finding too little?

- Choose another database.
- Check your query (spelling, date range).
- Reduce the terms or complication of query.

After you find a study, ask *Is the Study Right for YOU?*

- Is the language too complicated? (Do not reject too quickly—studies become easier to read.)
- Is the study too long? Look for a manageable size (between 5 and 10 pages, but can be longer).
- Is this a real study or is it a book review, letter to the editor, research note, feature, and so on? Look for the scientific study format (abstract, introduction, methods, results, analysis, conclusion, and references to identify a real study).
- Does the study topic help answer your research question? (Perhaps the answer is one you did not expect!)

Remember, there is no perfect study! You are looking for what science is currently saying about your topic, not what you think you should find about your topic.

From *Teaching the Scientific Literature Review: Collaborative Lessons for Guided Inquiry,* by Randell K. Schmidt, Maureen M. Smyth, and Virginia K. Kowalski. Santa Barbara, CA: Libraries Unlimited. Copyright © 2014.

Workshop 10

How to Read and Take Notes from a Peer-Reviewed Journal Study or White Paper

Overview

The Introduction to the scientific literature review (SLR) has been written and the student has begun the database search for peer-reviewed (PR) studies about the topics being researched. At this point, the student should have printed out two or more studies that should now be read and annotated to be included in the SLR. Remind the student that the SLR depicts what scientists are currently reporting about research that scientists have undertaken in the past few years. The student, therefore, is merely reporting on what scientists have said. His readings, annotations, and summaries should reflect what scientists are saying about the research, not what the student thinks about what the research says.

As the student begins to read the study, he should be reminded to look at the title, citation information, and abstract that appear before the text of the study. The student should use hard copy printouts of the study to highlight and annotate the information. Again, he should be reminded that the study is divided into sections: Abstract, Introduction, Methodology or Procedures, Results of Research, Analysis, and Conclusion. If the student's study is not similarly subtitled, the teacher or librarian should check the text to ascertain the nature of the student's article. He should also be reminded to avoid overextending himself and to choose studies that, although difficult, are readable and not of excessive length.

Please Note: This overview contains three sections of instructions for the teacher to pass on to the student: (1) The annotations made on each study, (2) the questions asked of each study or white paper as the student interrogates the text of the study or white paper, and (3) the citations required to responsibly account for borrowed information.

Annotations

Three types of annotations will be used in the PR articles. Each annotation taken should be succinct, as lengthy annotations tend to confuse the student researcher. Notes should be taken:

1. With a highlighter
2. With one- to four-word margin reminders of highlighted material
3. With two- to three-paragraph summaries in the student's own words, written directly after reading the material, *on the back page of the study's printout.* If quotations are used within the summary, special care should be taken to cite the page of the quotation.

Questions Asked to Interrogate the Study

As with the annotations for the Introduction section, the student is again encouraged to focus on information that is meaningful and important to him. The highlighting and margin annotations of the highlighted material (O'Connor, 1999) should also provide answers to the following questions about the study being read. Six main research questions asked by the student about the material are:

1. What is the question, controversy, or problem driving the study? (*Find in the Title or Introduction*)
2. Who or what group was being studied? Describe these people as much as possible, including their location(s), their characteristic(s), and their condition(s). (*Find in the Methodology or Procedures*)
3. How was the study executed? (What method was used, what kind of study was done?) (*Find in the Methodology*)
4. What questions were addressed or asked in the study to generate data? (*Find in the Methodology and Results of Research*)
5. What was found in the study? What were the results of the study? Why did the scientists think they found what they found? (*Find in the Results of Research and Analysis*)
6. After looking at the Results and Analysis, compare and contrast the studies. This comparison and contrast will become your analysis. Are they similar or different? What are the similarities among the studies and what are the differences? Are the questions driving the study similar? Are the groups studied similar or different? Are the results of the studies similar or different? Are there similar analyses of the findings? Are there trends in the various aspects of the studies, omissions, errors, or elements of the studies that are difficult to understand or rationalize? Write about this in your Analysis of Research.

The six questions listed above are the most important questions to ask of the information found in each study because the answers to the six questions comprise the text for the students' findings or what the student finds in the scientific literature he is reviewing. The student should be informed that this page is the most important page of the book because on this page are the questions the student must use to interrogate the studies and the location within each study where the answer to the question will be found.

The summary of two to three paragraphs per study should be written by the student immediately after the study has been read and annotated. The summary can fit very easily in handwritten form on the back of the last page of the study printout. **The student is required to use the back page because he is more likely to use his own words to paraphrase and summarize the information**. All material quoted should be clearly marked as a quote. Within the two to three paragraphs, the student should summarize the answers to the first five main research questions.

Of the six main research questions (O'Connor, 1999), answers to the first five (questions 1–5) will comprise the body of the text of the Results of Research section of the SLR. The answers to question 6 will comprise the body of the Analysis of Results section. The student should be reminded of the American Psychological Association (APA) requirements to cite all borrowed material.

Citations of Borrowed Information

While there is no consensus of a single stylistic standard on where to place a citation for borrowed material within the text of a SLR, we recommend a simple rule for citation placement. Information that has been borrowed from another author or authors and has been either paraphrased or summarized and paraphrased should be cited in the following way: The student should maintain a consistent application in the placement of the citation for borrowed material. The citation, which includes the author's last name, a comma, and the year of publication and is held in parenthesis, should be placed immediately after the first subject term of the sentence(s) referring to or using the borrowed material. Therefore, the citation is usually at the beginning of the paragraph after the subject term. Unless the student stops using the borrowed material or begins using material from another source, the citation holds until the end of that paragraph. If the next paragraph continues to use the borrowed material, a new citation must be added after the first subject term of the new paragraph. This citation will hold through the second paragraph. For a quotation of more than a few words, the APA style manual demonstrates the formatting of the quotation and the citation placement. For more information about citations, the student should be referred to the *Publication Manual of the American Psychological Association* (APA, 2010).

Organizing the text will be covered in **Workshop 12: How to Write the Results of Research**.

Workshop 10: How to Read and Take Notes from a Peer-Reviewed Journal Study or White Paper

Learning Goals: The goal of this workshop is for the student to locate the information that answers the six key research questions about the scientific study or the four key research questions found in a white paper, and compose a summary in his own words.

Location: Library

Team: Teacher, Librarian, and Resource Guide

Inquiry Unit: This workshop will provide the answers to the following questions: How can I read a study or white paper and make useful notes? How can I summarize information from my studies or white paper in a way that is scientific, relevant, and detailed?

Total Time: 50 minutes

Starter Time: 10 minutes	The goal of this workshop is to learn how to read and take notes from a peer-reviewed journal study or white paper. The teaching team will distribute and display Handout 1 and Handout 2. The teaching team will also circulate among the students to ascertain that each student has at least one or two printed studies or a study and a white paper. Any student who does not have the necessary documents should sit with the librarian or resource guide and obtain a study. The teaching team will ask the students to use a pencil or pen and a highlighter which should be passed out if needed. The teacher refers to the second page of the overview for **Workshop 10** which shows a list of six questions. The first five questions are used by the student to interrogate the text of the study. If a student has a white paper, the questions used to interrogate that text can be referred to in Handout 2. This workshop is about teaching the student to interrogate the text in such a way as to cull scientific information that is interesting to the student. The students will pull out a study and using Handout 1 or Handout 2 begin reading the study or a white paper, and as the article is read, begin highlighting the responses to the questions found in the study or in the text of the white paper.
Work Time Time: 35 minutes	Students will use the Handouts to guide them in answering the corresponding first five of the six research questions. Students should highlight information that is both interesting and relevant and make short annotations in the margin denoting why that information is important to the student. Each question should be answered on the back of the study in the student's own words. This text is the student's summary which later becomes the text of the body of the paper. Study summaries should be between two to three paragraphs. Some summaries may be longer. Students must include consistent in-text APA style citations in their summaries.
Reflection Time: 5 minutes	Students should discuss the significance of the research questions and the need to interrogate a text with those questions, instead of simply reading the text.
Notes	The recommended length of the summaries may be expressed in a range of paragraph numbers and/or word count (three paragraphs is the average target). The number of studies found, read, and summarized may vary according to the teaching team's requirements and course circumstances.

From *Teaching the Scientific Literature Review: Collaborative Lessons for Guided Inquiry*, by Randell K. Schmidt, Maureen M. Smyth, and Virginia K. Kowalski. Santa Barbara, CA: Libraries Unlimited. Copyright © 2014.

Common Core Standards	CCSS.ELA-Literacy.RST.11-12.1: Cite specific textual evidence to support analysis of science and technical texts, attending to important distinctions the author makes and to any gaps or inconsistencies in the account.
	CCSS.ELA-Literacy.RST.11-12.9: Synthesize information from a range of sources (e.g., texts, experiments, simulations) into a coherent understanding of a process, phenomenon, or concept, resolving conflicting information when possible.

Handout #1: How to Read and Take Notes from a Peer-Reviewed Journal Study

After reading your six general press articles on the subject you are studying, you have searched in a database which publishes *PR* scientific journal articles that are studies using terms that pertain to your research topic. You, then, find a list of several studies and choose one that you will read. The choice you make must be readable, that is, contain easy enough language and a style that you can make sense of. Now, you are about to discover how scientists report their research

What you do as you read the article describing a study is very important. Before you read the full text, thoroughly read the whole title of the study and the title of the journal in which the study is published; highlight this information. This will give you a general idea about the study you are about to read. Next, read the Abstract which is usually one paragraph in length and labeled *Abstract*. Then, check the text of the article. Is there an *Introduction, Methods,* or *Methodology* section, a *Results of Research* section, an *Analysis* or *Discussion of Research* section, and finally a *Conclusion*? Most published studies will be organized this way, with most or all the sections labeled as mentioned or with similar language. Most studies will also contain tables, charts, or graphs which graphically depict data from the study. To contain all of the above, most studies are *more than three* pages long—some are as long as 20 pages or more. Discard the excessively long study in favor of one that is under 10 pages, if possible. Then, print out your choice of a study so that you can read and take notes.

Do not go crazy with the highlighter. The questions, listed below, *should be answered*. These answers are an essential part of your results of research text. Highlight the answers as you find them, making short one -to four-word annotations in the side margin, reminding yourself what you have just highlighted.

Six main research questions (O'Connor, 1999) are:

1. **What was the question, controversy, or problem driving this study? (*Find in the Title or Introduction*)**
2. **Who or what group was being studied? Describe these people as much as possible, their location(s), their characteristic(s), and their condition(s). (*Find in the Methodology*)**
3. **How was the study executed? What method of study was used, what kind of study was done? (*Find in the Methodology*)**
4. **What questions were addressed or asked in the study to generate data? (*Find in the Methodology and Results of Research*)**
5. **What was found in the study? What were the results of the study? Why did the scientists think they found what they found? (*Find in the Results of Research and the Analysis*)**
6. **After looking at the Results, compare and contrast the studies. This comparison and contrast will become your analysis. Are they similar or different? What are the similarities among the studies and what are the differences? Are the questions driving the studies similar? Are the groups studied similar or different? Are the results of the studies similar or different? Are there similar analyses of the findings? Are there trends in the various aspects of the studies, omissions, errors, or elements of the studies that are difficult to understand or rationalize? Write about this in your Analysis of Research.**

After reading, highlighting, and annotating, turn over the study and write a summary of each study using the answers to the first five of the questions. Your summary should be two to three paragraphs long. The answers to questions 1–5 become the body of your *Results* section. The answer to question 6 will become the body of your *Analysis of Results* section. Please ask the librarians or teacher for help; we will make it easier for you to understand this assignment and finish the research paper.

Handout #2: How to Read and Take Notes from a White Paper

A. What Is a White Paper?

The SLR is a particular type of scientific study often completed by a scientist before undertaking a new experimental or observational study. In a SLR, a scientist will examine the existing already published studies to determine the breadth and depth of current research about his topic. By reviewing the current scientific literature, the scientist familiarizes himself with the information and is better able to formulate an updated pathway for his own new research.

When completing a SLR, the scientist will examine two types of PR journal materials: the scientific study which has already been described and the theoretical white paper. Both are published in PR journals for dissemination to the scientific community. The study depicts information found as a result of the scientific method and is written with that protocol in mind. A theoretical white paper is a document of an entirely different nature. It, too, is usually written by a qualified scientist whose training involves the subject matter in the white paper. But, unlike a study, a white paper often *precedes* or *replaces* a scholarly study.

The white paper depicts a theoretical or abstract yet substantive approach to a scientific question. A study describes how a scientific question was embodied, examined, measured, and analyzed in a real-life setting of a laboratory or field of experimental paradigm. Most studies are quantifiable or at least descriptive of concrete reality. A white paper, on the other hand, is an abstract (pre-real-life measurement) treatment of a scientific question, one which has not yet been studied or quantified because the scientific question is too new and the issues are just emerging or because science has not yet figured out how to study and quantify the measurement. Theoretical physics, for example, is a field of science that presently is sometimes difficult to experiment with because measurement of subatomic strings, for example, is not yet possible. A white paper is, therefore, written by someone scientifically trained, but the paper will be articulated in abstraction to examine a scientific question which has not yet lent itself to formal scientific inquiry.

B. Questions to Address the White Paper for the Scientific Literature Review

A white paper is a theoretical paper but not a study, sometimes published in a PR journal and written by an expert or authority in the field being studied. A white paper examines some aspect of a topic which might be studied in the future. White papers are sometimes written to discuss a condition, problem, controversy, or question that scientists will research at some point in the future.

If you are using a white paper in the literature review, find the answers to the following 4 questions:

1. **What is the problem, controversy, or question being examined?**
2. **How is the scientist looking at the problem, controversy, or question in the white paper?**
3. **What description or categories does the scientist use in his paper?**
4. **What proposals or possible new ideas about the topic does the white paper suggest?**

Use these questions in place of the five questions you address to the studies. Write your summary paragraphs out of the answers to these questions.

From *Teaching the Scientific Literature Review: Collaborative Lessons for Guided Inquiry*, by Randell K. Schmidt, Maureen M. Smyth, and Virginia K. Kowalski. Santa Barbara, CA: Libraries Unlimited. Copyright © 2014.

Research in the Formulation Stage of the Information Search Process

Workshop 11: How to Write the Methodology

Unlike other less complex research papers or projects, the scientific literature review involves the processing of a large amount of highly sophisticated information in a relatively short period of time. Students have been informed and reminded that several hours of searching, reading, and summarizing scientific studies are a requirement of the workshops. In this formulation stage, those hours have been completed and the student must now sift through all that information to find the patterns of the results of her research and begin to internalize the meaningful information to identify a research question that the information addresses. Now, in identifying or formulating the focus or question of the studies, the student should begin to articulate, with the help of the Teaching Team, the research question being addressed in the literature review.

Workshop 11

How to Write the Methodology

Overview

This lesson provides the student with an explanation of why a Methodology is included in a scholarly paper and why the Methodology is particularly important when writing about science. To avoid confusion, explain that the Methodology is sometimes referred to as the Procedures section. By either name, this section describes how the research (the study) was conducted. As such, the Methodology provides the reader with the steps the researcher used to develop her research.

The student researcher begins to write her Methodology by stating that she conducted a scientific literature review (SLR) of the topic researched. This statement is followed by a verbal pathway to the general press (GP) articles and scientific studies (PR) employed to develop the SLR. Included in this pathway are the titles of all the GP article sources, all scientific journals used, the search terms utilized to find the articles and studies, the databases searched, and the dates of access to the databases for the materials.

The teacher can inform the student that it is standard practice in the scientific arena for the author to indicate how and where she retrieved the data. This is vital not only because other scientists can ascertain the currency and establish the validity of the research, but also so that others can replicate, use, and build upon the scientific information presented.

Scientific research protocol requires that research be replicable, thus providing continuity within the subject under scientific investigation and establishing accountability for the scientific work. In reality, the Methodology is the impetus to further scientific research, and therefore plays a crucial role in expanding exploration within the scientific community. A teacher might also want to inform the student that the Methodology is generally the shortest part of the SLR, consisting of approximately two paragraphs. This knowledge of brevity might prove beneficial in keeping the student focused on the task at hand.

A Methodology section is very structured. It contains two paragraphs that include information about where the GP and peer-reviewed (PR) studies were found, the dates of publication, databases used, search terms employed, and when these materials were accessed. Each of the two paragraphs that comprise the Methodology is broken up into approximately six sentences. Paragraph one concentrates on those GP articles that point out what the world is saying about the student's topic.

To begin, the student indicates that a SLR was conducted to examine her research subject. Sentence two lists the names of all the GP sources used in the research, indicating those newspapers, magazines, or other sources consulted for the Introduction. Sentence three specifies the chronological range of the publication sources used. Please note that as with all scientific writing, currency is an important factor; therefore, the teacher should suggest the student remain within a five-year range of the year the SLR is being written, if possible. In sentence four, the student then goes on to indicate the databases or other information delivery systems used to retrieve the information. In sentence five, the search terms used to retrieve the GP articles are listed. Each search term is indicated by quotation marks and separated by commas. In sentence six, the final sentence of the first paragraph specifies the dates that the student accessed the materials from the databases or other electronic sites. The student should be informed that the access date for both GP and PR articles must be indicated in the SLR and that access date information can often be found at the bottom of the article printout.

Paragraph two concentrates on those scientific PR journal studies that focus on what scientists are studying and saying about the student's topic. The studies are used to develop the Results of Research section and, later, the Analysis of Research section of the SLR. Again, the formatting is organized in a very methodical sequence. Sentence one begins by stating that scientific, peer-reviewed journals were used to develop the main body of this literature review. The student then continues, in sentence two, to list all the journals consulted to locate the PR studies. These journals should be written in the order they appear in the Results section and typed in italics. In sentence three, the researcher indicates the dates all the PR studies were published, from the earliest date to the latest date, again adhering to the five-year span of publication. Sentence four points out the databases used to conduct the research, while sentence five indicates the search terms used to retrieve the studies. Again, each search term is written in quotation marks and separated by commas. Finally, sentence six in paragraph two of the *Methodology* section includes the dates these PR studies were accessed from the databases.

Please see the student handout for "How to Write the Methodology." Using the handout and materials contained in the student's research folder, the Methodology section can be drafted during one class period.

Reminder: If the class has been using an online bibliography generator (see **Workshop 6: Starting the Reference List**), the student should have already begun entering the titles and information about her sources.

Workshop 11: How to Write the Methodology

Learning Goals: The goal of this workshop is for the student to understand why methodology reporting is needed in scholarly research and to compose the methodology section of the research paper.

Location: Library

Team: Teacher and Librarian

Inquiry Unit: This workshop will provide the answers to the following questions: What is an information/research pathway? How is methodology reporting relevant to my research? How can I write a Methodology?

Total Time: 50 minutes

Starter Time: 5 minutes	The goal of this workshop is to provide students with an explanation of a methodology section in scientific scholarly research, so that the student understands what is required for scientists to ascertain the currency and establish the accountability and replicability of research. The student is expected to complete most of the methodology during this workshop. Scientific research protocol requires that research be replicable, thus providing continuity within the subject under scientific investigation and establishing accountability for the work. The teacher can inform the student that it is standard practice in the scientific arena for the author to indicate how and where she retrieved the data, thus describing the scientific method. Using general press (GP) and peer-reviewed (PR) sources, the teaching team should point out the bibliographic or reference citation section of each GP and PR article which shows the student all the information needed for the reference entry. Teachers ask the students to compose their methodology using Handout 1 and the librarian will review each section of the methodology which the student must complete.
Work Time Time: 40 minutes	Students will use Handout 1 to guide them as they compose the methodology. The teaching team can circulate in the room and assist students with finding the proper citations in each article, study, or white paper, as the formatting for each may differ. Students will locate the information from their articles and studies and fill in the blanks on the given handout. Once the form is complete, students can type the handout if time permits.
Reflection Time: 5 minutes	Students may discuss the importance of scientific accountability and replicability. The students and teaching team may discuss why scientific information pathways are important and how the student can ride the citation wave for her own research using reference lists and literature review methodologies. Students may also discuss why it now makes sense to diligently organize and highlight source material in each article, study, or white paper for easy citation retrieval, and input for both the methodology and on-going bibliography/reference list.
Notes	Students should, provided they have on hand all GP and PR articles, be able to complete the methodology in one workshop period. If the student is unprepared, a one-on-one tutorial should be scheduled with the librarian.

From *Teaching the Scientific Literature Review: Collaborative Lessons for Guided Inquiry,* by Randell K. Schmidt, Maureen M. Smyth, and Virginia K. Kowalski. Santa Barbara, CA: Libraries Unlimited. Copyright © 2014.

Common Core Standards	CCSS.ELA-Literacy.W.11-12.1d: Establish and maintain a formal style and objective tone while attending to the norms and conventions of the discipline in which they are writing
	CCSS.ELA-Literacy.W.11-12.1a: Introduce precise, knowledgeable claim(s), establish the significance of the claim(s), distinguish the claim(s) from alternate or opposing claims, and create an organization that logically sequences claim(s), counterclaims, reasons, and evidence.
	CCSS.ELA-Literacy.RST.11-12.9: Synthesize information from a range of sources (e.g., texts, experiments, simulations) into a coherent understanding of a process, phenomenon, or concept, resolving conflicting information when possible.

Handout: How to Write the Methodology

The Methodology section of your SLR consists of two paragraphs.

Paragraph I: Introduces your topic and explains how and when you found materials for your Introduction.

Sentence 1: A Scientific Literature Review was conducted to examine _____. (*Your research subject*)

Sentence 2: The introductory material was found in the following general press sources: (*List and italicize the names of ALL the newspapers, magazines, documentaries, etc. used.*) _____, _____, _____.

Sentence 3: All general press articles were published since _____. (*Earliest year only*)

Sentence 4: Searches for information were conducted in the following databases: _____, _____, and _____.

Sentence 5: Search terms for GP articles included: "_____," "_____," and "_____."

Sentence 6: Dates of access to introductory materials were: _____/_____/_____, _____/_____/_____, _____/_____/_____ and _____/_____/_____.

Paragraph II: Explains how and where you found studies and scientific information for the main body of your paper.

Sentence 1: Scientific peer-reviewed journals were used for the main body of this literature review.

Sentence 2: The journals consulted include: _____, _____, and _____. (*List and italicize the names of ALL the journals used.*)

Sentence 3: All peer-reviewed studies were published from _____ to _____. (*Earliest date/latest date*)

Sentence 4: All studies were found in: _____, _____, and _____ databases.

Sentence 5: Search terms used to search for studies include: "_____," "_____," and "_____."

Sentence 6: Dates of access to peer-reviewed articles were: _____/_____/_____, _____/_____/_____, _____/_____/_____ and _____/_____/_____.

Hints: On the bottom of your article printout, you may find the date of access. The source author and source information will be on the top of the printout, next to the volume and issue number of the journal. If in doubt, check by redoing a search or ask the librarian for help. Be specific in the keywords/ search terms listed; this is a part of your grade!

From *Teaching the Scientific Literature Review: Collaborative Lessons for Guided Inquiry*, by Randell K. Schmidt, Maureen M. Smyth, and Virginia K. Kowalski. Santa Barbara, CA: Libraries Unlimited. Copyright © 2014.

Assessment Rubric: Methods of Research

The Methods of Research is worth a maximum of 10 points toward the final grade.

10–9 points = Demonstrates excellent understanding of methods of research through the use of multiple, varied, and timely sources.

8–6 points = Demonstrates good understanding of methods of research through the use of multiple, varied, and timely sources.

5–0 points = Demonstrates incorrect or insufficient understanding of methods of research through the use of limited, irrelevant, or obsolete sources.

Points are awarded for the following:

Criteria	Points Earned

Use of General Press Articles
(Worth 4 points)
• Six to eight relevant general press articles used for introductory material
• Includes:
  ○ Source titles
  ○ Publication range
  ○ Databases used
  ○ Search terms used
  ○ Dates of access or DOI	

Use of Scientific/Peer-Reviewed Journals
(Worth 4 points)
• Six to eight studies used (white paper, if librarian approved)
• Includes:
  ○ Source titles
  ○ Publication range
  ○ Databases used
  ○ Search terms used
  ○ Dates of access or DOI	

Methodology *(Worth 2 points)* • Methodology is introduced using accurate scientific format provided	
Total Points for the Methods of Research: *(Maximum 10 points)*	

Research in the Collection Stage of the Information Search Process

Workshop 12: How to Write the Results of Research
Workshop 13: How to Use and Create a Table, Chart, or Graph for the Research
Workshop 14: How to Write the Analysis of Research

During the Collection Stage, three workshops are conducted and detailed. All three workshops are interdependent and should be completed in sequence. During the Collection Stage, the student is discerning which data drawn from the studies read are most useful and how the data can best depict a review of the recent literature.

To use a simple analogy, at the point of the Collection Stage, the student has a pile of pieces of information. The student must collect from that pile the pieces that best reflect the research done and adequately respond to his research question. Once he has found those pieces of information, he must create a visual representation to help him analyze what the information means. His analysis marks the end of the Collection Stage.

Workshop 12

How to Write the Results of Research

Overview

As Wernher von Braun said, "Basic research is what I'm doing when I don't know what I'm doing." For an idea to coalesce in a student's mind, from vague speculation, through theory and finally crystallize into knowledge, requires not only imagination and investigation, but hard work and practice. The ability to compile and compare results is the cornerstone of science and can be achieved only by the repetition of experiments and the evaluation of the different outcomes. Research provides us with a map of the paths through the intricate forest. Only after considerable research can we focus on and genuinely appreciate the true beauty of an individual tree. (John Taeschler, Chemistry Teacher, Gill St. Bernard's School, 2007)

At this point in the research process, the student is probably gaining confidence that the assigned paper can be completed. And, in fact, he should be reminded that the bulk of the research work is done now that the studies have been found, read, annotated, and summarized. Now, the job is to organize the results and transcribe the summaries into the Results of Research section. Again, the student should be reminded that as he composes this section he is merely a science reporter, providing information that has been discovered from recent scientific studies. The student/reporter is not, at this point, commenting on that information. The Results of Research section of the scientific literature review (SLR) will reveal studies read, methodologies used and described in the studies, findings of the studies, and analysis of the findings reported in each study. Once the Results of Research section is completed, the majority of the paper is done. The student researcher sometimes gets carried away and begins to insert opinions and ideas into the Results that are not reflected in any of the studies. Such editorializing must be avoided.

Each study's set of results must be reported. Students will need guidance on how to unite the summaries of the different studies. Suggested organizational tactics include:

1. Topically—Separate the studies into topics or subjects examined in the research.

2.   Chronologically—Indicate first study conducted to last study or last study to first.
3.   By group studied—Put studies in order by who was studied. Was it:

   • All age groups?
   • Different ethnic groups, ages, occupations, or socioeconomic groups?
   • Different genders?
   • Geographic locations?
   • Situations and/or conditions?

4.   By questions asked in the study—Examine what was studied and how.

This is obviously not a comprehensive list. Teachers and librarians should assist students in deciding the best organization for the SLR. No one scheme fits all. However, in a democratic society, science shoulders a responsibility to all citizens. If the participant body in a group of studies within a literature review is exclusive to only a portion of those affected by the condition or problem being studied, then the scientific community is not reflecting diversity. Students should be reminded that groups studied may reflect a comprehensive scientific investigation if, as a sum, the groups studied are an inclusive representation of a given population. However, if the groups studied are an exclusive representation of a given population which is affected by the condition or problem being studied, that exclusivity may inadvertently reflect bias.

After an organizational scheme has been chosen, titles should be attached to the sections or subsections of the Results. An example of an introductory sentence for the Results of Research could read: *A Scientific Literature Review was conducted to examine the effects of pesticides. Six studies were reviewed and categorized in the following manner:*

1.   Pesticides' effects on farm workers—(three studies in this group)
2.   Pesticides' effects on children of farm workers—(one study in this group)
3.   Pesticides' effects on school children eating fruits and vegetables—(two studies in this group)

As this limited example illustrates, the organization of the Results of Research essentially depends on the nature of the studies found and upon the results contained in those studies. Students should understand there is no right or wrong way to write up the Results of Research.

The student should walk away from the instruction for writing the Results of Research section, knowing that the section is about the information found in the studies and not about what the student thinks of that information.

How to Write the Results of Research—this is the largest section of the Scientific Literature Review. Even though the peer reviewed studies were extremely long, I already had a set of assigned questions for each study. This made it much easier because each study was already summarized into the five main questions whose answers would be used in the Results of Research. The most difficult part of the Results was figuring out the order I would use when talking about each study. I had to figure out which studies were similar so the Result's information would flow. I learned how to take good notes when it comes to reading something really long. Instead of taking notes on everything, which sometimes makes me take notes on the least important information, I learned how to break information down into those things that were more important. I had to make sure I answered each of the five questions thoroughly in order to have a successful Results Section. I also had to make sure the information I used was relevant to my topic at all times. Even though this was the largest paper I ever wrote, it was made less difficult as we completed it section by section. At the same time, I was well prepared organizing all the information needed to construct a successful paper. (Karen Arias, Student, Gill St. Bernard's School, 2007)

Workshop 12: How to Write the Results of Research

Learning Goals: The goal of this workshop is for the students to organize the findings of the literature review into an effective report of research.

Location: Library

Team: Teacher, Librarian, and Resource Guide

Inquiry Unit: This workshop will provide the answers to the following questions: What is the purpose of the Results of Research section of a SLR? How can I organize and effectively present my research? How can I tie together the findings of the six studies?

Total Time: 50 minutes

Starter Time: 10 minutes	The goal of this workshop is to prepare a report of the six studies into a cohesive paper. The teaching team will pass out examples of professional scientific literature reviews. The class will discuss possible ways to organize each study's set of results by creating a simple model student literature review that is rather outlandish. For example, a suggested student review might be six studies on student hair treatment preference. One study might examine teenage hair color preferences. Another study might examine hair length and style in teenagers. Two other studies might examine girls' hair coloring for the prom. And the last two studies might examine motivation for shaving part or all of the head. Using this example of a literature review, the librarian can suggest organizational tactics to report the findings. The findings could be reported topically, chronologically, by groups studied, or by questions asked in the study, among other possible options. The student should be reminded that his efforts in this workshop will result in an organized text for his paper.
Work Time Time: 30 minutes	The teaching team will ask the students to decide among the tactics which way the student will choose to report the six studies. Students will be reminded that this is a scientific endeavor and that they are reporting, not editorializing, the findings. The students will then make those decisions, as the teaching team circulates around the room answering questions and helping students decide how to report the findings.
Reflection Time: 10 minutes	Students can offer their potential reporting tactics with comments and questions from their peers. Students may reflect upon the effort it takes to organize and effectively present the research.
Notes	While it is quite possible in one 50-minute workshop to determine how to tie together and report findings, many students may need other nonstructured workshop time, and indeed some tutorial one-on-one time assistance.

| Common Core Standards | CCSS.ELA-Literacy.RST.11-12.9: Synthesize information from a range of sources (e.g., texts, experiments, simulations) into a coherent understanding of a process, phenomenon, or concept, resolving conflicting information when possible.

CCSS.ELA-Literacy.W.11-12.4: Produce clear and coherent writing in which the development, organization, and style are appropriate to task, purpose, and audience. (Grade-specific expectations for writing types are defined in standards 1-3 1-3 above.)

CCSS.ELA-Literacy.WHST.11-12.1c: Use words, phrases, and clauses as well as varied syntax to link the major sections of the text, create cohesion, and clarify the relationships between claim(s) and reasons, between reasons and evidence, and between claim(s) and counterclaims.

CCSS.ELA-Literacy.WHST.11-12.1d: Establish and maintain a formal style and objective tone while attending to the norms and conventions of the discipline in which they are writing. |

Handout: How to Write the Results of Research

Your six or more studies are now annotated and summarized. No changes have to be made in your summaries. The summaries should answer the first five main research questions asked in **Workshop 10: How to Read and Take Notes from a Peer-Reviewed Journal Study or White Paper** of the text. If they do, then the summaries **become** the results of research, in need only of transitions between the summaries. The summaries are the text for your Results of Research section. You may organize this Results section in one of several ways, including but not limited to:

1. Topically—Separate the studies into topics or subjects examined in the research.
2. Chronologically—Put in order from first study conducted to last study or last study to first.
3. By group studied—Put in order by who was studied. Was it:

   - All age groups/different age groups?
   - Different ethnic groups?
   - Sexes/gender identities?
   - Geographic locations?
   - Situations and/or conditions?

4. By questions asked in the study—Examine what was studied and how.

After you have placed these studies and their summaries in groupings, label each group and create a narrative using your annotations and summaries for each. Here, you use the annotations that answer questions 1–5 on your "How to Read and Take Notes from a Peer Reviewed Journal Study" sheet. You are not offering your opinions about each study; instead, you are a scientific reporter. You are letting the details of the study (particularly the answers from questions 1–5) speak for themselves. This section is only about the studies and the answers to the main research questions.

The best way to organize the summaries is to spread them out in front of you. Read all the summaries together. After you have refreshed your memory, make a brief annotation about the essential nature of the study. Either annotate on top of the summary or on a post-it note those summaries that share characteristics of subjects examined, groups studied, similar methods, and so on. Group your summaries and label them with the shared group characteristic(s). Physically, put together the studies as you will present them in your paper from first to last. After you have the summaries grouped, use them as the text of your narrative, connecting the summaries' text with transitional language.

Use objective, factual language, and tone. Avoid pronouns (e.g., we, they, I) and *never* say I think, I believe, or I feel. It is not about you—it is about the information found and what the studies are saying.

Assessment Rubric: Results of Research

The Results of Research is worth a maximum of 10 points toward the final grade.

10–9 points = Demonstrates excellent understanding of results of research through the precisely, accurate, well-organized, and comprehensive summarization of the research.

8–6 points = Demonstrates good understanding of results of the research through the accurate and organized summarization of research.

5–0 points = Demonstrates incorrect or insufficient understanding of results of the research through limited and/or poorly organized summarization of research.

Points are awarded for the following:

Criteria	Points Earned
Citation of Scientific/Peer-Reviewed Journal Studies *(Worth 6 points)* • At least six to eight relevant peer-reviewed scientific journal studies used • Well summarized • Proper use of APA format	
Organization *(Worth 2 points)* • Results of research are easy to read • Subtitles are utilized	
Mechanics and Grammar *(Worth 2 points)* • Correct spelling • Correct grammar • Use of objective/factual language	
Total Points for the Results of Research: *(Maximum 10 points)*	

From *Teaching the Scientific Literature Review: Collaborative Lessons for Guided Inquiry*, by Randell K. Schmidt, Maureen M. Smyth, and Virginia K. Kowalski. Santa Barbara, CA: Libraries Unlimited. Copyright © 2014.

Workshop 13

How to Use and Create a Table, Chart, or Graph for the Research

Overview

The old saying that "a picture is worth a thousand words" holds true in science as well. Sometimes, the best way to depict dense or important information is graphically rather than textually. In the scientific literature review (SLR), the author (student) is employing a graphic display such as a table, chart, or graph to illustrate some aspect(s) of the results of the research. For example, a student reporting on research about eight different studies of dyslexia and cognition may decide to create a table that shows the studies used, listing the age groups studied, the main question the studies examined, and a key finding of each study. This table is an easy tool that can organize and display studies, methodologies, and some findings. A chart or graph can also be used to pinpoint specific data from individual studies or to compare specific data from two or more studies examined in the SLR.

Students should be reminded that no one table, chart, or graph can stand in the place of an accurately written narrative in the SLR. The table, chart, or graph can, however, highlight or emphasize key findings or important comparisons among the studies being reviewed. The student should understand that graphically displayed material placed within the Results of Research section of the paper should echo part of the text of that section and not be used in place of, or instead of, the text.

Our experience in teaching the SLR has shown that a useful table can be created by the student that pinpoints key information gleaned from each of the first five main research questions from **Workshop 10**. Thus, the table will list the six studies reviewed on the top horizontally and the five questions asked vertically with a column for each study and a box for each main research question used. The student will then fill in the boxes, one study at a time, putting one or two key pieces of information in each box. (See student's example in **Handout #1.**)

When the table is complete, the student has a one- to two-page visual representation and is able to compare and contrast the information found for each of the main research questions. Thus, she is able to analyze the findings between the studies. All graphic displays must be properly titled and clearly labeled and be original to the student's SLR. The student should not copy any graphics found within any studies being reviewed. Rather, any table, chart, or graph created to depict the results of the SLR must be the student's original work.

Workshop 13: How to Use and Create a Table, Chart, or Graph for the Research

Learning Goals: The goal of this workshop is for the student to create a table to visually represent a portion of a body of research and to use the table to construct the analysis of research section. The secondary goal of this workshop is for the student to understand the function of a table, chart, or graph in representing some of the information found in the study.

Location: Library/Computer Lab

Team: Teacher, Librarian, and Resource Guide

Inquiry Unit: This workshop will provide the answers to the following questions: What is the purpose of a table, chart, or graph in a scientific research paper? How can I create a research table? What elements can I use to create a graphic display of findings?

Total Time: 50 minutes

Starter Time: 15 minutes	The goal of this workshop is to provide students with a tool to create a graphic display of findings. Handout 1 should be distributed to students. To illustrate the lesson, the teaching team could create a prototype table or use the example in Handout 2. Students are given a blank table template to create a visual representation of their research. Students will use the table, for the purpose of this assignment, to help them write the analysis section of the paper. The table will help students to further chunk the research findings information into concise, more obvious divisions. Vertical columns represent each individual study, while horizontal rows represent the answers to the main research questions found in **Workshop 10: How to Read and Take Notes from a Peer-Reviewed Journal Study or White Paper.** Prior to constructing the analysis, the student should be informed that she will refer to the table as she looks for similarities, differences, trends, omissions, and errors in the research. The teaching team can remind students not to overload the table, instead focusing on the most important information to the student and not everything in the study.
Work Time Time: 30 minutes	The student will create a table using the template found in Handout 2. The student should place in front of her the summaries of the six studies. She will then insert the information from each study which answers the first five research questions she has paraphrased in the summary. The teaching team will circulate throughout the room to assist individual students. Should one or more students need additional help, fellow students may be called upon to explain the table or a tutoring session should be arranged for one-on-one teacher to student assistance.
Reflection Time: 5 minutes	Students should discuss why a table, chart, or graph might help them to visually understand the comparison of the studies.

Notes	The table is complex and the assignment is long. Therefore, at least one more unstructured workshop should be allotted for the completion of the table. Individual students may need extra help. The librarian and science teacher may decide not to make a table, chart, or graph a required element of the scientific literature review. The lesson can be taught in conjunction with **Workshop 12: How to Write the Results of Research.**
Common Core Standards	*CCSS.ELA-Literacy.WHST.11-12.1b*: Develop claim(s) and counterclaims fairly and thoroughly, supplying the most relevant data and evidence for each, while pointing out the strengths and limitations of both claim(s) and counterclaims in a discipline-appropriate form that anticipates the audience's knowledge level, concerns, values, and possible biases. *CCSS.ELA-Literacy.WHST.11-12.1c*: Use words, phrases, and clauses as well as varied syntax to link the major sections of the text, create cohesion, and clarify the relationships between claim(s) and reasons, between reasons and evidence, and between claim(s) and counterclaims. *CCSS.ELA-Literacy.WHST.11-12.2a*: Introduce a topic and organize complex ideas, concepts, and information so that each new element builds on that which precedes it to create a unified whole; include formatting (e.g., headings), graphics (e.g., figures, tables), and multimedia when useful to aiding comprehension.

Handout #1: How to Use and Create a Table, Chart, or Graph for the Research

Tables, charts, and graphs can help you summarize, describe, document, or highlight one or more specific aspects of your results (not the entire study). They will help you convey your message by presenting and illustrating your findings in a visual manner. The reader may look at these illustrations before reading the complete text to get a feel for the paper. Therefore, the table, chart, or graph should reflect an important example of data.

- Tables—Data is arranged in columns and rows, essentially in a rectangular form. The label goes above the table. If possible, confine each table to a single page for easy review of the information.
- Charts and Graphs—Charts and graphs are used to illustrate quantitative relationships. They are often used to make it easier to understand large quantities of data and the relationship between different parts of the data. Charts and graphs can be read more quickly than the raw data, which provides the basis of the graphic display.

Elements of a Successful Graphic Display

Tables, charts, and graphs should be simple and easy for the reader to understand. They should be clear, concise, accurate, and memorable. If you choose to illustrate some of your data, remember that *you* create the table, chart, or graph. You do not simply borrow a graphic from one of the sources you have accessed and read. Tables, charts, and graphs should be referred to and explained in the text of your *Results* section. They should be sufficiently complete to stand on their own and be somewhat understood apart from the text. They must be titled and numbered consecutively.

How to Create a Graphic Display for Your Paper

1. *Decide what to say.* Think of your graphic the way a magazine editor might think about the cover photo. What is the big story in your paper? You may want to zero in on an element of your analysis of studies that is powerful, fascinating, or surprising. You may want to focus on the most important data you found. You may choose to present the big picture, a graphic that organizes and summarizes the main aspect(s) of all your studies. You may wish to compare an element shared among your studies. However, your graphic cannot show everything.
2. *Decide how to say it.* What graphical organization best lends itself to the story you wish to tell? Is it a numbers story? A chart or graph may allow you to simplify complex and large numbers. Play around with various formats.
3. *Present it clearly and accurately.* Your graphic must precisely reflect the information in the studies you utilized. It is easy to become confused, as you transfer numerical data and other information. Check your information and properly cite your sources. Does your graphic speak for itself? Can your reader understand the information?
4. *Explain it concisely.* Look at your *Results*. Does the graphic zero in on a specific point? Can it become more powerful with editing?
5. *Place it in your paper.* Does the graphic connect to your *Results* section? Is it your original work? Is it titled and numbered with citations?

Table: Comparisons of effects of dyslexia in eight studies

	Study #1 Citation: Boets & De Smedt, 2010	Study #2 Citation: Klein & Verwey, 2009	Study #3 Citation: Ferrari et al., 2007	Study #4 Citation: Aladwani & Shave, 2012	Study #5 Citation: Kirby et al., 2010	Study #6 Citation: Dror et al., 2010
Questions driving the study	Do dyslexic children struggle with math?	How do different types of learning affect students with dyslexia?	What are the effects of learning disabilities on learning a foreign language?	How much knowledge do teachers have about dyslexia?	What are the study skills of dyslexic children?	What are the benefits of linear vs. nonlinear note taking?
Groups studied	29 third graders with dyslexia and 25 without, all were native Dutch speakers	40 students from Saxon college, 19 with dyslexia all native Dutch speakers	152 7th and 8th grader Italian students, all attending a public junior high	English and Arabic primary school teachers of all different backgrounds and degrees	College level students from 4 different schools, all students were diagnosed with dyslexia, a control group was also used	Men and women ranging from 24 to 59 years old who were experienced in their work field
Methods	Flashing of problems by putting math problems on a board	Computer test used colored boxes that the participant was told to press the correct one	Student read passages and read questions out loud to test accuracy and speed	Surveys were used that asked about background and personal info and knowledge. 75 students	Self-tests were used, and a reading passage with multiple choice questions, also a questionnaire. 102	Watch 2 different videos and take notes, some using linear and some using nonlinear, then fill evolution 33

Figure 1

Source: Sample table was created by Hannah Geldzahler–2013.

Some examples of research findings in pictorial or graphic forms

Pie Chart

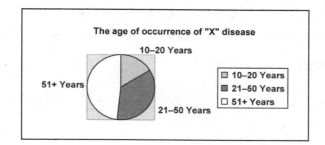

Figure 2

Graph

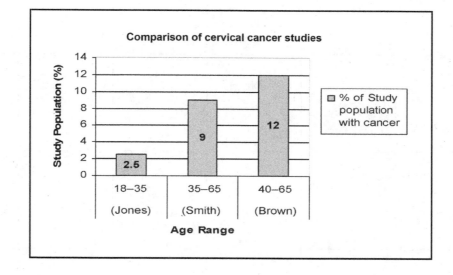

Figure 3

Source: The sample Chart and Graph were created by Josie Muench who was instrumental in designing this workshop.

From *Teaching the Scientific Literature Review: Collaborative Lessons for Guided Inquiry*, by Randell K. Schmidt, Maureen M. Smyth, and Virginia K. Kowalski. Santa Barbara, CA: Libraries Unlimited. Copyright © 2014.

Handout #2: Template for Student-Generated Research Table

	Study #1 Citation:	Study #2 Citation:	Study #3 Citation:	Study #4 Citation:	Study #5 Citation:	Study #6 Citation:
Questions driving the study						
Groups studied						
Methods						
Findings—Results of each study						
How was the study analyzed? (Why did the researchers think they found what they found?)						
Recommendations (include any omissions)						

From *Teaching the Scientific Literature Review: Collaborative Lessons for Guided Inquiry*, by Randell K. Schmidt, Maureen M. Smyth, and Virginia K. Kowalski. Santa Barbara, CA: Libraries Unlimited. Copyright © 2014.

Workshop 14

How to Write the Analysis of Research

Overview

As a science teacher reading and grading a research paper, it is in this section where I can get a very good sense of how well the student is understanding the material. In this section the really good papers become evident. Here the student goes beyond the basic reporting of the peer reviewed studies. Here he will, hopefully, be able to see various connections between the studies. Students should be able to note and write about certain trends. Are there contradictions in the conclusions or do they concur? The students should discuss if the studies used similar methods to reach their conclusions. If for, example, groups of people were studied, were these groups of similar size and demographics? If questionnaires were used, how were the questions phrased, and in what form were they presented; in phone interviews or face-to-face sessions, etc. (Michiel Stil, AP Bio/Biology Teacher, Gill St. Bernard's School, 2007)

The student is now reaching a critical stage of the research process in which an analysis of the research found in the scientific literature review (SLR) must be undertaken and written up. Until now, the student has primarily filled the role of research reporter or scientific scribe searching for, finding, annotating, and summarizing the work of other writers and scientists who are (through general press and scientific publications) informing the world about "real-time" science.

Now, it is the student's turn to use the publications found and summarized in the Results of Research section. This peer-reviewed (PR) scientific information about recent studies must be put on the table and scrutinized by the student to determine several aspects of the science being reported. Examining all the studies together for comparison and contrast will help the student go beyond reporting and begin to synthesize the information. The student will combine the heretofore uncombined information to discover similarities, differences, trends, gaps, contradictions, and omissions between and among the different study information sets.

The student should be made aware that this stage of the paper requires him to think critically and to respond with his own original thoughts. We are now asking the student for a personal response, not an uninformed opinion but a response informed by scientific information, a response that critically (scientifically and as objectively as possible) examines various aspects of the studies and presents the student scientist's unique understanding of the whole body of studies reviewed by analyzing the particulars.

Writing the analysis of research is the moment when the student engages in the creation of new knowledge, for the student is not merely reporting the differences or similarities between the studies. The student is thinking about and analyzing **what, why, or how** those differences and similarities are and what they mean for the topic he has chosen to research. Science reporting gives way to critical analysis, as the individual student thinks about the information found in the research.

The results of the studies have become the raw material for an original analysis by the student, because the student may be the only individual on earth reviewing the particular studies he has chosen. This is his own review of the data he analyzes, which he has chosen from all the data found in each study. The student now truly "owns" his analysis.

The process of synthesis thinking which comes from comparing and contrasting the data leads to the creation of some of the student's own ideas about the information being examined. The ownership of those newer ideas produces a deep, more sophisticated understanding of the subject being researched. And because the subject being researched stems from a personal question originally cast by the student researcher, the information gleaned, compared, and contrasted becomes more meaningful as a response to the personalized question. The meaningful response to the initial personalized question produces a memorable impression and deeper knowledge.

The student should be reminded here that just as he previously interrogated specific sections of the study text to find specific answers to the first five main research questions, from **Workshop 10: How to Read and Take Notes from a Peer-Reviewed Journal Study or White Paper**, now he must also interrogate the study as a whole, up against the five or more other studies reviewed to determine the efficacy and replicability of each study.

The student handout "How to Write the Analysis of Research" provides six tips on writing the *Analysis of Research* section. Remind the student that all tips should be considered; other tips may be added. All studies must be included in the *Analysis of Research* section, although some may provide more information and detail than others. The analysis each student completes should include comparisons between the studies (see horizontal boxes in the analysis table) and comparisons within each study (see vertical columns within the analysis table).

Like many of the lessons given by Mrs. Schmidt for the Junior Research Project one in particular was very helpful to me. I decided to research the Causes and Effects of Homelessness in America and the biological aspects of this. Upon hearing that an Analysis section was required in this paper, I was very confident that I knew what I was going to write and that this section would be the easiest, but when I sat down to write this paper I was very confused and did not understand exactly what I was analyzing. When Mrs. Schmidt gave us the lesson on *How to Write Up Your Analysis Of Research Section*, and broke it down for us giving us specific things to incorporate in this section, I found it to be a lot easier for me.

I found it less difficult, because I had guidelines to follow and as long as I made sure that I did each step using the checklist that was given to me in the lesson I did not leave anything out. I also found it to be quicker to write because I no longer had to put unnecessary things into my paper. I knew exactly what I was going to write about. The Analysis section required me to look at each study and compare them. I needed to compare studies based on the methodologies used, the questions that drove the studies and the results found in each study. Knowing this I knew exactly what I was to look for in my peer reviewed studies. I was amazed that I did not even have to re-read the studies because of the notes that I had taken on all the studies.

I began to realize that the lessons that Mrs. Schmidt gave us and the guidelines we had to follow taught us not only how to complete that specific section, but it also prepared us for sections to come. I recognized this when it came time for me to write my Analysis section and was grateful for the lessons that we had received. (Tempestt Duncan, student, Gill St. Bernard's School, 2007)

Workshop 14: How to Write the Analysis of Research

Learning Goals: The goal of this workshop is for the student to compare and contrast information and discover similarities, differences, trends, omissions, and errors in the body of the six studies which constitute the student's literature review.

Location: Library or Classroom

Team: Teacher, Librarian, and Resource Guide

Inquiry Unit: This workshop will provide the answers to the following questions: What is the purpose of the Analysis of Research section of a science research paper? How can I compare and contrast six studies? How can I effectively develop and present my analysis of research?

Total Time: 50 minutes

Starter Time: 10 minutes	The goal of this workshop is to create the student's own analysis of the six or more studies reviewed. This analysis takes the form of comparisons and contrasts between similarities, differences, trends, omissions, and errors found among the studies. The teaching team will distribute the Handout and introduce the workshop by having the student pull out the table he has created, which in a concise way indicates the findings of all the studies. One student can volunteer his table to be used as a model. The librarian, using the information from the table and making columns and rows on a whiteboard, will then point out the similarities, differences, trends, omissions, and errors by comparing first the questions driving the study, followed by the groups studies, methods employed, results of research, and why the researcher thinks he found what he found.
Work Time Time: 30 minutes	The students will begin using the table to compare the question driving each study and determine through comparisons and contrasts the similarities, differences, trends, omissions, and errors among the studies. The teaching team will circulate to assist and spot check the progress of the students. Midway through the work time, students should begin comparing in more detail the group(s) studied in each scientific study the student has read. While the student may have answered the previous question of what was driving the study with only one statement, the question of who or what group(s) was studied demands a description of several characteristics of the group(s) studied. Again, the teaching team should circulate to assist and spot check the progress of the student. The same process extends to the Methodology, Results, and Analysis of each study.
Reflection Time: 10 minutes	Beyond the comparisons and contrasts of similarities and differences, in the individual sections of the paper, students should discuss how to distinguish omissions, errors in the studies, and trends for future research. The reflection could begin with the teacher asking the students to identify one future study each student's literature might suggest and why.
Notes	At least two more unstructured work times should be allotted for students to complete the analysis and for the teaching team to assist in that completion.

From *Teaching the Scientific Literature Review: Collaborative Lessons for Guided Inquiry*, by Randell K. Schmidt, Maureen M. Smyth, and Virginia K. Kowalski. Santa Barbara, CA: Libraries Unlimited. Copyright © 2014.

Common Core Standards	CCSS.ELA-Literacy.WHST.11-12.1b: Develop claim(s) and counterclaims fairly and thoroughly, supplying the most relevant data and evidence for each, while pointing out the strengths and limitations of both claim(s) and counterclaims in a discipline-appropriate form that anticipates the audience's knowledge level, concerns, values, and possible biases.
	CCSS.ELA-Literacy.WHST.11-12.2b: Develop the topic thoroughly by selecting the most significant and relevant facts, extended definitions, concrete details, quotations, or other information and examples appropriate to the audience's knowledge of the topic.
	CCSS.ELA-Literacy.WHST.11-12.2c: Use varied transitions and sentence structures to link the major sections of the text, create cohesion, and clarify the relationships among complex ideas and concepts.
	CCSS.ELA-Literacy.WHST.11-12.2d: Use precise language, domain-specific vocabulary, and techniques such as metaphor, simile, and analogy to manage the complexity of the topic; convey a knowledgeable stance in a style that responds to the discipline and context as well as to the expertise of likely readers.

Handout: How to Write the Analysis of Research

Your analysis incorporates all the studies you found and may be approximately 1½ to 5 pages long. In your analysis, you are looking at each study as a whole against other studies as a whole. In order to do the comparisons of similarities, differences, trends, omissions, and errors and to make recommendations for future studies, however, you must first make sense of why the question driving the study was addressed to the group studied and how the group studied influenced the methodology employed for the study. You must think if the results found in the studies were influenced by the questions asked, the groups studied, and the methods used. Use your table of the five main research questions as your guide for your analysis and look at each vertical column for a summary of each study. Then, compare the information between the studies by looking at each horizontal row, as each row depicts the findings among the studies for each of the first five main research questions from **Workshop 10: How to Read and Take Notes from a Peer-Reviewed Journal Study or White Paper**.

1. Look at your six or more studies.
2. Examine the answers to questions 1–5 in your study's summary notes (two to three paragraph write-ups about the studies). Look at the whole study by looking down the vertical column. Does the study hold together? Does it seem like good science? Could it be repeated and get the same results?
3. Now, look across the horizontal rows to compare the same aspect in each of the different studies.

    a. Compare the question(s) driving each study.
    b. Compare the group(s) studied.
    c. Compare the methodologies used.
    d. Compare the findings of each study, what results each study provides.

4. Examine how each study was analyzed. Did the aggregate of the studies you read leave out some obvious aspects of possible research? What should be the focus of the next wave of research about the subject?
5. When you are comparing the studies, see if each makes sense to you, and if the study seems to be consistent with the question driving the study. Ask yourself what is similar in any of the studies and what is different. Question if the study can be easily replicated and if the findings make sense in relation to the questions asked. Ask yourself if anything has been omitted from the studies. Question whether the several groups studied are representative of a target population.
6. Be sure to cite each study when you refer to it in your analysis. You must also cite with each new paragraph that refers to any borrowed information.
7. Remember, this is the section of the paper that calls for you to think about the information you have encountered and reported thus far. This is *your* analysis of other scientists' research.

From *Teaching the Scientific Literature Review: Collaborative Lessons for Guided Inquiry*, by Randell K. Schmidt, Maureen M. Smyth, and Virginia K. Kowalski. Santa Barbara, CA: Libraries Unlimited. Copyright © 2014.

Assessment Rubric: Analysis of Research

The Analysis of Research is worth a maximum of 10 points toward the final grade.

10–9 points = Demonstrates excellent understanding of the topic through comprehensive comparisons between studies, trends, and research shortcomings.

8–6 points = Demonstrates good understanding of the topic through some comparisons between studies, trends, and research shortcomings.

5–0 points = Demonstrates incorrect or insufficient understanding of the topic through limited use of comparisons between studies, trends, and research shortcomings.

Points are awarded for the following:

Criteria	Points Earned
Comparisons (*Worth 4 points*) Comparisons are made between the studies by: • Populations studied • Question driving each study • Methodologies used • Study results	
Analysis (*Worth 4 points*) After looking at the research results, does the analysis examine: • Similarities or differences among existing research • Obvious omissions • Errors • Contradictions between the results • Potential for future research	
Mechanics and Grammar (*Worth 2 points*) • Correct spelling • Correct grammar • Use of objective/factual language	
Total Points for the Analysis of Research: (*Maximum 10 points*)	

Research in the Presentation Stage of the Information Search Process

Workshop 15: How to Write the Conclusion
Workshop 16: How to Write the Abstract
Workshop 17: Creating a Title and Completing the Cover Page

Research in the Presentation Stage involves three workshops which are detailed herein. At this point of the information Search Process, the student has already determined what the literature review will cover, her research question has been articulated, and she will add **no new information** to her text. The conclusion and abstract are both brief recapitulations of her literature review. The student has now processed a sufficient amount of information to objectively and accurately title her scientific literature review. These three workshops represent the culmination of the research project and produce the final sections of text to fully present the research accomplished.

Workshop 15

How to Write the Conclusion

Overview

The function of the Conclusion of the scientific literature review (SLR) is to summarize the study undertaken. Thus, the Conclusion serves as a brief recapitulation of the information already presented in the first four sections of the research paper: Introduction, Methodology, Results of Research, and Analysis of Research. As a summary, it is a reiteration, and it introduces no new information, comment, or analysis but merely states briefly, once again and in the SLR author's own words, what the SLR is all about.

Writing such a Conclusion—especially for students accustomed to writing humanities papers, in which a Conclusion may contain important new information or analysis—is a difficult undertaking. A formulaic approach is possible, though not required, to fulfill the obligation. One such formula can be found in the handout "How to Write a Conclusion."

Finally, students should once again be reminded that multiple and accurate citations must be included in the Conclusion for *any* and *every* reference to information borrowed by the student from a reviewed article, study, or white paper. In fact, the Conclusion may have more citations per paragraph than any other section, as the student attempts to distill and summarize the literature review into a few paragraphs. Every reference to an article, a study, a finding in a study, or to an analysis of a study should include a citation of that study. The conclusion will have two or three sentences summarizing each section of the paper. The Conclusion will likely have several citations for each study used. The entire conclusion will be 1 to 1½ pages long.

Workshop 15: How to Write the Conclusion

Learning Goals: The goal of this workshop is for the student to understand the structure and format of a conclusion in a scientific research paper.

Location: Library or Classroom

Team: Teacher, Librarian, and Resource Guide

Inquiry Unit: This workshop will provide the answers to the following questions: Why is a conclusion necessary in a scientific paper? How is a conclusion relevant to my research process?

Total Time: 50 minutes

Starter Time: 5 minutes	The goals of this workshop are to provide students with an explanation of a conclusion in scientific scholarly research and for the students to understand how to write a conclusion. Using a sample conclusion, the teaching team can walk students through the formulaic approach to the conclusion. Students should be reminded that no new information is necessary for the conclusion and that the conclusion should be brief—between 1 and 1½ pages. Multiple and accurate citations must be included for any and every reference to borrowed information. Each study or white paper used will require several citations. In fact, the conclusion may have more citations per paragraph than any other section, as the student attempts to distill and summarize the literature review into a few paragraphs. Librarians will distribute the handout. Teachers ask the students to compose their conclusion using the Handout. The teaching team will assure the students that assistance is available as they write their conclusions.
Work Time Time: 40 minutes	The student will use the Handout to guide her, as she writes this final section of the scientific research paper. The teaching team should circulate to monitor students and ensure that they are including accurate citation placement and not introducing any new information.
Reflection Time: 5 minutes	Students can discuss how the conclusion fits into the process. What does the conclusion mean to the student's research? And why should the student not include any new information in the conclusion? How is this conclusion different from the conclusion in a humanities paper?
Notes	The conclusion should be drafted during the workshop. However, students may need more time to polish their writing. Tutorial aid should be offered.
Common Core Standards	*CCSS.ELA-Literacy.WHST.11-12.1e*: Provide a concluding statement or section that follows from or supports the argument presented. *CCSS.ELA-Literacy.WHST.11-12.2e*: Provide a concluding statement or section that follows from and supports the information or explanation provided (e.g., articulating implications or the significance of the topic).

Handout: How to Write the Conclusion

The Conclusion

A Conclusion is merely a brief summary of your paper. You must not introduce any new materials, ideas, or information in your Conclusion. However, you must cite within the text of the Conclusion any study, idea, or information you refer to again.

Writing Your Conclusion

Because the Conclusion is just a *brief* summation of the different parts of your paper, below is a formula you may use to write it:

1. Write two sentences in your own words to summarize your Introduction, borrowing others' information and ideas. Here, each general press (GP) article will be represented by a phrase and a citation.
2. Write two sentences in your own words to summarize your Methodology. Here, you name your own methodology (a scientific literature review) and you list all of your sources.
3. Write two to three sentences in your own words (borrowing others' information and ideas) to summarize the Results section. Here, each study will be represented by a phrase and a citation.
4. Write two to three sentences in your own words (borrowing others' information and ideas) to summarize the Analysis of Research. Here, all the similarities, differences, trends, omissions, errors, and suggestions for future research will be noted briefly, if possible, and all studies cited as they are noted.

All sentences should reference and cite sources, information, and ideas you found within the material you borrowed from the general press (GP) (for the introduction only) and the scientific studies (PR) (for the rest of the paper). *Do not forget* to cite any and all information that you borrowed and used in your Conclusion section. If your research is extensive and you have written more than three sentences per section, try to be as concise as possible.

Now, you have completed the Conclusion in your own words!

Assessment Rubric: Conclusion

The Conclusion is worth a maximum of 10 points toward the final grade.

10–9 points = Demonstrates excellent understanding of the topic through comprehensive comparisons between studies, trends, and research shortcomings.

8–6 points = Demonstrates good understanding of the topic through occasional comparisons between studies, trends, and research shortcomings.

5–0 points = Demonstrates incorrect or insufficient understanding of the topic through limited use of comparisons between studies, trends, and research shortcomings.

Points are awarded for the following:

Criteria	Points Earned
Summary *(Worth 8 points)* The summary includes: • Two sentences summarizing the Introduction • Two sentences summarizing the Methods of Research • Two to three sentences summarizing the Results of Research • Two to three sentences summarizing the Analysis of Research • No new ideas are represented • Proper citations for each study referenced	
Mechanics and Grammar *(Worth 2 points)* • Correct spelling • Correct grammar • Correct APA format	
Total Points for the Conclusion: *(Maximum 10 points)*	

Workshop 16

How to Write the Abstract

Overview

Every high school and college student should know how to write an Abstract, how to read an Abstract, and what function an Abstract serves in the worlds of science and information. This lesson provides students with an explanation of why an Abstract is attached to a scholarly paper, and why an Abstract is so important to student research and to research in general.

A student-generated Abstract functions in the same way as an Abstract in a scholarly paper: It briefly summarizes the research and provides search terms for locating that research. By introducing the Abstract as a "shortcut" tool for focused information searching, it suddenly becomes more useful and more interesting to the student. When a student carefully composes his own Abstract, a deeper understanding of the database search process is possible. Each Abstract is constructed by the scholar using key terms or subject terms that summarize each section of his research. These terms lead researchers to that paper because they precisely and directly represent the content of the research. By searching in the text of the Abstract only, a scholar will be able to conduct a more precise and concise information search in a database that houses published studies with Abstracts. Abstract searching is easier, provides more useful information, and saves time because it helps locate only specific subject matter described by the subject terms in the Abstract.

An Abstract may be explained to the student as a one-paragraph summary of his paper. According to the *Publication Manual of the American Psychological Association* (APA, 2010), it should be no longer than 250 words. It may not, however, be a summary familiar to most students. The Abstract is really a paragraph of sentences filled with nouns that identify what the research covers. An Abstract is a fairly commonplace element in database articles. However, like the source information included at the top of each article entry, it is often overlooked or not understood by students. Most students are unaware of the ease and precision of searching by Abstract and most are not familiar with its function as a descriptive narrative of the research paper or presentation.

Students may be told, "When you write your Abstract, you are writing an information pathway into your paper." **For this paper, however, the abstract should be no more than 150 words.**

Teaching students how to compose an Abstract should be one of the last lessons of the research program because the Abstract's composition requires that the Introduction, Methodology, Results of Research, Analysis, and Conclusion be available for summary in the Abstract.

A student who learns how to write an Abstract is learning how to write like a scientist. A good Abstract allows other people to see what the paper describing a study is about. It is written more for the benefit of other scientists who want to discover what is in the paper. As a brief synopsis of the results of the study, the Abstract is like a whole paper in only one paragraph. The Abstract presents a brief, non-emotional, to-the-point, concise rendition of a scientist's research. (Michiel Stil, AP Biology teacher, Gill St. Bernard's School, 2007)

Workshop 16: How to Write the Abstract

Learning Goals: The goal of this workshop is for the student to understand how to structure and compose an abstract for a scholarly literature review.

Location: Library or Classroom

Team: Teacher, Librarian, and Resource Guide

Inquiry Unit: This workshop will provide the answers to the following questions: What is the purpose of an abstract? How do I conduct a search using an abstract? How can I write my abstract with as many keywords as possible?

Total Time: 50 minutes

Starter Time: 5 minutes	The goal of this workshop is to provide students with an explanation of an abstract in scientific research and to begin to compose the abstract. Students are asked to use Handout 1 to list keywords and subject terms from the student's collection of studies and white papers. The librarians will explain again the significance of keyword searching in database research and the resulting textual nature of the abstract. Students should understand that the best abstract consists of as many keywords as can be placed reasonably within a paragraph abstracting the research. The teaching team should encourage the student to review each study or white paper and look for margin annotations and keywords noted in the summaries. Using Handout 1 and Handout 2, students should include a list of keywords covering the questions asked in the study, groups studied, methodologies employed, and results of research. The teaching team should remind students to use nouns and formal scientific language. The student should be specific and brief as the abstract must be no more than 150 words.
Work Time Time: 40 minutes	Students will use Handout 1 to guide them in listing keywords and subject terms for the abstract. Students will need time to review their summary notes and tables to refamiliarize themselves with the specifics of each study.
Reflection Time: 5 minutes	Reflection should focus on what is the function of an abstract? How can the student use an abstract as a shortcut tool for his own research in the future?
Notes	The number of key terms required for this assignment may be fine-tuned to reflect numerous circumstances, including available time for projects, student abilities, the number of studies required, intended final paper length, and so on.
Common Core Standards	*CCSS.ELA-Literacy.WHST.11-12.2d*: Use precise language, domain-specific vocabulary and techniques such as metaphor, simile, and analogy to manage the complexity of the topic; and convey a knowledgeable stance in a style that responds to the discipline and context as well as to the expertise of likely readers. *CCSS.ELA-Literacy.WHST.11-12.2e*: Provide a concluding statement or section that follows from and supports the information or explanation provided (e.g., articulating implications or the significance of the topic).

From *Teaching the Scientific Literature Review: Collaborative Lessons for Guided Inquiry,* by Randell K. Schmidt, Maureen M. Smyth, and Virginia K. Kowalski. Santa Barbara, CA: Libraries Unlimited. Copyright © 2014.

Handout #1: How to Write the Abstract

The Abstract

Abstracts are written so that scholars and information searchers can easily access *precise* articles, studies, and white papers about a subject of interest. Information is concisely described in the Abstract. Abstracts promote access to information by containing as many distinct and varied subject terms as can be used in approximately one paragraph. One hundred fifty words or less should adequately describe the subject(s) of the literature review.

An Abstract is an important tool to reduce the work of searching for appropriate information. When you are hunting for published information, search in the Abstract first as you will be better able to pinpoint substantive information about your subject or related subjects rather than merely searching the whole text of an article.

When you write your Abstract, remember that others who are searching are looking for information on subject terms that describe your research. Be *precise, varied*, and *accurate* in the subject terms used. Use as many subject terms as possible (at least 20), but be precise.

Writing Your Abstract

A good way to begin writing your Abstract is to take a blank sheet or use **Handout 2: The Abstract Generator** worksheet and write down a list of 20–30 subject terms that come to mind when you think of your research. In this list, try to include about 15 terms describing the studies and 15 terms describing the findings of the studies.

Tips for Generating Your Subject Terms

- Remember to use NOUNS.
- Use scientific, formal language (personality disorder NOT bad personality).
- Be specific and brief (leukemia NOT various forms of cancer).
- Look at the keywords/search terms of your studies.
- Use more than one word if needed.

Good examples from previous papers, if available, will be distributed so that you can see a student-prepared Abstract. Or, if you look at some of the scientists' Abstracts in the studies you have read while doing your own research, you will find other examples of Abstracts to use as models.

Please ask if you have any questions! The librarians are glad to help you.

Handout #2: Abstract Generator

My Abstract Generator: Key Terms List

To begin writing your *Abstract*, write down a list of 20 or more subject terms that come to mind when you think of your research. You can use this list to write your *Abstract*!

Step I. Generate Terms

Terms describing the studies (the question driving the study, groups studied, and method of study):

Questions:

1.   4.

2.   5.

3.   6.

Groups:

1.   4.

2.   5.

3.   6.

Methods:

1.   4.

2.   5.

3.   6.

Terms describing the findings of the studies:

1.   9.

2.   10.

3.   11.

4.   12.

5.   13.

6.   14.

7.   15.

8.

Step II. Write Your Abstract

As you begin to write your *Abstract*, review the five sections of your paper. Then, explain briefly, using your 20+ subject terms, what you found in your literature review. Reflect on the concepts and organization of your paper. Be sure to list your study as a scientific literature review. Use your own words but avoid casual or slang language. Keep the language academic! The *Abstract* should be one paragraph and no more than 120–150 words long.

Assessment Rubric: Abstract

The abstract is worth a maximum of 10 points toward the final grade.

10–9 points = Demonstrates excellent understanding through consistent use of good term selection and organization

8–6 points = Demonstrates good understanding through frequent use of good term selection and organization

5–0 points = Demonstrates incorrect or insufficient understanding through the limited use of good term selection and poor organization

Points are awarded for the following:

Criteria	Points Earned
Number of Terms (*Worth 5 points*) • 20 or more terms	
Term Selection (*Worth 2 points*) Terms are consistently: • No more than 150 words • Precise • Varied • Accurate • In noun form • Reflect scientific/formal language	
Mechanics and Grammar (*Worth 2 points*) • Correct spelling • Correct grammar • Correct APA format	
Organization (*Worth 1 point*) • Abstract consistently reflects the content and organization of the paper	
Total Points for the Abstract: (*Maximum 10 points*)	

Workshop 17

Creating a Title and Completing the Cover Page

Overview

The student is nearing the end of the research process and must cap her scientific literature review (SLR) with a properly prepared Title and Cover Page. This workshop is self-explanatory and the worksheet given to the student says it all.

The Title contains a succinct description of the student's topic of scientific research. A student's Title should be composed in a straightforward informational manner and should sound formal and professional in its tone. It should be produced by each student but the teacher may assist the student by asking the student to summarize in one sentence the key aspects she learned in the literature review. Other features of the Cover Page are discussed and the student is directed to an APA style manual to view an example of the composition of the Cover Page.

For the purpose of brevity and paper conservation and for this assignment, the Abstract is also placed on the Cover Page as per instructions in **Workshop 16: How to Write the Abstract.**

*Please note that combining the Cover Page with the Abstract is a departure from American Psychological Association (APA) style guidelines.

Workshop 17: Creating a Title and Completing the Cover Page

Learning Goals: The goal of this workshop is for the student to create a title and complete an appropriate cover page for a scholarly paper.

Location: Library or Classroom

Team: Teacher, Librarian, and Resource Guide

Inquiry Unit: This workshop will provide the answers to the following questions: What is the purpose of a title for a scientific research paper? How can I write a clear and concise title for the research paper? And what other information goes on my Cover Page?

Total Time: 50 minutes

Starter Time: 10 minutes	The goal of this workshop is to formulate a title and create an appropriate cover page for a scholarly paper. The teaching team calls for two or three student volunteers to read their abstracts aloud to the class, one at a time. Having heard the abstracts, the librarian will suggest possible scholarly titles based upon the contents of the abstract. Usually, the title involves either a cause and effect or a disease/disorder and related treatments or some sequencing of the studies reviewed. After the examples are examined and written on the board, the students break into pairs to work on individual titles. Prior to breaking into groups of two, the teaching team will distribute the Handout and display examples of an APA style title page which, for this paper, will also include the abstract. Samples can be given to students of a cover page with a title and an abstract.
Work Time Time: 30 minutes	Students will decide in the study pairs on a possible title for each paper. The teaching team will circulate to confer with students about the possible title and approve or guide the students' suggestions. The teaching team can assist the novice researchers with the type of scientific language used in scholarly writing for completing the abstract. Students can then work to merge the abstract they have written with a title and proper heading. On the bottom right hand corner of the cover page, the student will add her name; underneath her name will be the course name; the third line will contain the teacher's name; and finally the date of submission. Here is an example: Sarah Brown Advanced Placement Biology Mr. Stil/Mrs. Schmidt March 7, 2013 A header containing the first word of the paper's title (which is not an article) and the page number will be added to the top right-hand corner of each page of the SLR beginning with the cover page. The librarians should explain that this formatting for the cover page differs from the traditional APA cover page and includes the abstract of 150 words or less.

Reflection Time: 10 minutes	Students can share their titles with the class and receive constructive comments.
Notes	The teaching team can provide extra unstructured work time for completion of the cover page. This workshop may be combined with **Workshop 16: How to Write the Abstract** due to its brevity.
Common Core Standards	*CCSS.ELA-Literacy.W.11-12.10*: Write routinely over extended time frames (time for research, reflection, and revision) and shorter time frames (a single sitting or a day or two) for a range of tasks, purposes, and audiences. *CCSS.ELA-Literacy.W.11-12.2e*: Establish and maintain a formal style and objective tone while attending to the norms and conventions of the discipline in which they are writing.

Handout: Creating a Title and Completing the Cover Page

The *Title* of your paper does more than name your Scientific Literature Review (SLR). The *Title* provides a reader with a single phrase or one-line synopsis of what you have been researching for these many weeks. It also provides a database searcher (assuming the literature review is eventually published in a journal and collected in a database) with a key to the information contained in the literature review. These are reasons to think carefully about the *Title* of your paper after the paper has been written. Generally, the researcher titles the paper. You may ask the science teacher or librarian for assistance.

Certainly, the *Title* should contain the key subject term(s) that relates to the research. For example, if the research just completed is all about Attention Deficit Disorder (ADD), then the *Title* should contain the three words "attention deficit disorder." To continue with this example, the student should ask herself what aspects of attention deficit disorder the (SLR) paper is focused on. Perhaps, the scientific literature reflected causes of ADD or perhaps the literature reflected cognitive results of the disorder. The student creating her *Title* should include in the *Title* what aspects were studied about the topic.

As the *Title* is considered, the student should examine the titles of some or all the scientific studies contained in her own SLR. The student should note that the language of the *Title* is formal and leads the reader right into the heart of the research currently being conducted about the topic.

A good *Title* stands alone and needs little explanation—it should not be cute, folksy, clever, or particularly creative. Instead, the *Title* should be a precise and concise rendering of the nature of the material contained in the SLR. A *Title* can also contain a subtitle which speaks more specifically to the subject studied. A *Title* should be straightforward and free of value judgments or personal bias, if possible.

After the *Title* has been written and inserted on the cover sheet in the location recommended by the APA style manual, the rest of the *Cover Page* information must also be composed and placed as per the APA guidelines. Included is the running page header which is the *first word of your Title* and the page number. In the case of the cover page, that number is 1.

Information to be placed on the *Cover Page* on the bottom right-hand corner includes the name of the writer/researcher of the SLR. This is followed by the name(s) of the course(s) for which the paper is being researched, the name(s) of the professor/teacher(s) teaching the course(s), and the date the paper is being turned in.

Finally, each SLR should contain an *Abstract* which has been described in **Workshop 16: How to Write the Abstract**. In a departure from the APA guidelines, insert the *Abstract* under the *Title* in the center of the page. After the *Abstract* is inserted and centered under the *Title*, the *Cover Page* is complete.

Your work is almost done!

From *Teaching the Scientific Literature Review: Collaborative Lessons for Guided Inquiry,* by Randell K. Schmidt, Maureen M. Smyth, and Virginia K. Kowalski. Santa Barbara, CA: Libraries Unlimited. Copyright © 2014.

Research in the Assessment Stage of the Information Search Process

Workshop 18: Putting It All Together to Hand Over the Scientific Literature Review to the Teacher

While assessments can be made throughout the Information Search Process, the *final* assessment is made after the student hands in his scientific literature review (SLR) paper and research folder. The final paper is prepared in two stages: the draft and the corrected final paper. A workshop is given to prepare the draft and the materials that must be presented with the draft, so that the teacher can correct the draft against the research documentation. After the corrected draft and documentation have been returned to the student, it is the student's turn to prepare his corrected final paper and turn in that paper and the research documentation in a research folder for a grade. The Teaching Team may also schedule a final workshop (not specified herein) for an in-depth reflection of the SLR process and the Guided Inquiry approach.

Workshop 18

Putting It All Together to Hand Over the Scientific Literature Review to the Teacher

Overview

The long-awaited time has arrived—the student's journey is over! The student's scientific literature review is complete, corrections have been made, and three final copies are ready to submit. The student must submit his research file twice during the research process. The first time the student turns his paper in to the librarian he should include all his research information and *three copies* of his draft for research content and citation corrections. The folder must contain copies of all research materials organized as indicated in the student handouts for this Workshop 18, Handout 1, and Handout 2.

The copies of the draft will go to the content teacher, the librarian, and one will remain uncorrected in the folder. All other material will remain in the folder for reference by the correcting librarian. Materials should be arranged as the handout suggests so they can be easily located by the correcting librarian.

After the draft is corrected, the librarian returns the student's folder, still containing all the research materials. The unmarked draft and one corrected copy of the draft will be returned to the student along with any other comments, if necessary. The content teacher marks his copy with first draft and retains that copy.

The folder is turned in a second time after the student has completed all corrections to the draft and now has a complete final copy of his paper.

Again, three clean, unmarked final copies are submitted along with the corrected first draft and all research materials organized as per the student Handout 1 and Handout 2 for Workshop 18. At this point, the research folder has become the student's completed learning portfolio for the project, and both the science teacher and librarian still have a lot of evaluative work to do.

Clean copies of final papers should be placed within a binder and prominently displayed for public perusal within the library. The benefits of these papers extend beyond the science classroom and serve as indications of the serious research being conducted at the school. Below is a representation of the value of displaying the SLRs:

Selling a school is a tricky proposition. In a business where sincerity is at a premium, prospective parents are very adept at realizing when someone may simply be telling them what they want to hear. Independent schools share some commonalities, small classrooms, engaging teachers, and beautiful grounds are the norm rather than the exception. However, there are programs that set the schools apart. The most common question I am asked by prospective parents and students is, "How is your program different from other schools in the area?" While I will never speak poorly of another program, I will always begin my description of what makes Gill St. Bernard's great with an in-depth overview of the research program.

When I first arrived at Gill St. Bernard's four years ago I was eager to meet with any teacher who was willing to explain his/her program. All the teachers were very accommodating and helpful, but it was a presentation by our head librarian that particularly interested me. Randi Schmidt came into the conference room and blew me away with her program. She explained the progression of the guided inquiry research program as it evolves over the four year high school career of the student, and how the student is empowered with information at the completion of his time at Gill St. Bernard's.

I was skeptical about the program being as good as Randi claimed it to be until I was invited to review the SLRs at the completion of the research process. I was inspired to see not only high quality work, but also the student's interest level in the project. Each student seemed to take clear ownership of the project and displayed a tremendous amount of professionalism in presenting the material.

In addition to my work in the admission office, I am currently pursuing a Masters in Education degree at Columbia University. Having graduated college from Hamilton College, a school known for producing sound writers, I felt confident in my abilities. That is until I received my first paper back. While stylistically my paper was fine, the professor was disappointed in the quality of my research. After showing the assignment to Ms. Schmidt she dropped everything she was doing and proceeded to give me an hour tutorial on database manipulation and primary source literature. Needless to say, my professor was impressed with my improvements. I tell this story often to prospective parents to illustrate the level of work their children can actually produce. Randi even joked with me that if I need help in the future and she was not around, just grab any junior who has completed a scientific literature review and he would be able to assist me!

The Guided Inquiry Research Program is a major reason our students succeed. The program sounds ideal in theory to prospective parents in the admission process. However, the true value is that the program delivers on the promise it makes that any student will be able to go into any library in the world and perform scholarly research. (Matt Marsallo, Admissions Officer, Gill St. Bernard's School, 2007)

For the student, now is the time of great relief and rejoicing. The research work is over! The SLR is complete!

Workshop 18: Putting It All Together to Hand Over the Scientific Literature Review to the Teacher

Learning Goals: The goal of this workshop is for the student to organize the research file and produce the draft and final paper copies of the SLR. Organization is needed to turn the paper and documentation in the research folder to the teacher and the librarian.

Location: Library

Team: Teacher and Librarian

Inquiry Unit: This workshop will provide the answers to the following question: How can the student organize the research file and provide the necessary documentation along with the paper, in order for the initial draft to be corrected and the final paper to be turned in and graded?

Total Time: 50 minutes

Starter Time: 10 minutes	The goal of this workshop is for the student to prepare his research file and paper for submission and review. The student will submit his paper twice during the research process. First, the student will turn in his research folder with three copies of his draft for research and content corrections. The student should include copies of all research materials organized, as directed in Handout 1 and Handout 2. Materials should be arranged as the handouts suggest for ease of location of materials by the correcting librarian. Second, the student will turn in three copies of the final research paper as well as the corrected version of the draft and all related research material. **This workshop applies to the first draft submission.** Along with three copies of the draft paper, students will include all handouts in the research folder and electronic printouts for general press articles and scientific studies Student handouts should be kept in chronological order in the *left pocket* of the folder. The *right pocket* should contain all materials collected for the scientific literature review. Students should mark all general press articles as GP and all scientific studies as PR and place them in the right pocket of the research folder in alphabetical order by the lead author's last name. Students should highlight bibliographic information on all GP and PR printouts. Students will need ample floor or table space to organize the research folders.
Work Time Time: 30 minutes	Students will use Handout 1 and Handout 2 to guide them as they organize all handouts and research materials. The student should have ample space either on a work table or the floor to spread out the contents of the research folder and reorganize according to the handout. The teaching team should circulate with copious supplies of paperclips, a stapler, and binder clips. Research folders in poor condition should be replaced. Names should be displayed on the front of each folder. Students should check a partner's folder.
Reflection Time: 10 minutes	Upon completion of the organizing task, the teaching team should ask the questions, "Why does the documentation have to be available for the paper to be graded?" "Why must it be organized?" Students may also reflect on the feelings they have upon completion of a significant project.

From *Teaching the Scientific Literature Review: Collaborative Lessons for Guided Inquiry*, by Randell K. Schmidt, Maureen M. Smyth, and Virginia K. Kowalski. Santa Barbara, CA: Libraries Unlimited. Copyright © 2014.

Notes	While it may have been evident prior to the workshop, the lack of a first draft at the time of this workshop will be the most definite indication of a student's need for extra help and tutorials. Often, this same student's need has already surfaced and teachers have been working with him to catch up with the rest of the class. However, now it is more pressing that the student is consulted and extra help is arranged.
Common Core Standards	*CCSS.ELA-Literacy.W.11-12.4*: Produce clear and coherent writing in which the development, organization, and style are appropriate to task, purpose, and audience. (Grade-specific expectations for writing types are defined in standards 1–3 above.) *CCSS.ELA-Literacy.RST.11-12.10*: By the end of grade 12, read and comprehend science/technical texts in the grades 11–CCR text complexity band independently and proficiently.

Handout #1: Checklist for Putting the Research Folder and Paper All Together

All handouts, paper copies of articles and studies, electronic printouts for general press (GP) articles and scientific studies (PR), and all drafts of your paper must be kept in this folder.

Contents of the Left Pocket:

Handouts should be kept in chronological order in the *left pocket* of the folder. The arrangement should be as follows:

Checklist for Handouts: 1 2 3

1. *The Benefits of a Scientific Literature Review* ____
2. *The Student's Assignment Begins* ____ ____ ____
3. *Making It Meaningful: Browsing Databases/Finding Information* ____ ____ ____
4. *Creating and Organizing the Research Folder* ____ ____ ____
5. *Researching the Introduction* ____
6. *Starting the Reference List* ____ ____
7. *How to Read and Take Notes from a General Press Article* ____
8. *How to Write an Introduction* ____
9. *Searching for Peer-Reviewed Studies* ____
10. *How to Read and Take Notes from a Peer-Reviewed Journal Study or White Paper* ____ ____
11. *How to Write the Methodology* ____
12. *How to Write the Results of Research* ____
13. *How to Use and Create a Table, Chart, or Graph for the Research* ____ ____
14. *How to Write Your Analysis of Research* ____
15. *How to Write the Conclusion* ____
16. *How to Write Your Abstract* ____ ____
17. *Creating Your Title and Completing the Cover Page* ____
18. *Putting It All Together to Hand Over the Scientific Literature Review to Your Teacher* ____ ____

Contents of the Right Pocket:

The *right* pocket should contain all the materials collected for the SLR.

Please mark all general press articles as GP and all scientific studies or white paper as PR and place them within the right-hand pocket of your research folder in alphabetical order by first author's last name.

Highlight bibliographic information on all GP and PR printouts.

Handout #2: Your Research Folder Contents

Your Research Folder/Portfolio	
Left Pocket	**Right Pocket**
[ ] All 18 workshop research handouts.	[ ] Six or more general press articles with highlights, annotations, and summaries.
[ ] Corrected copy of first draft. Should contain all of teacher's notes and corrections.	[ ] Six or more peer-reviewed scientific studies with highlights, annotations, and summaries.
[ ] Final paper—three clean copies (completely corrected and unmarked).	

Checklist:—Your draft and final papers should include: (all in APA style)				
Cover Page with Abstract [ ]	Introduction [ ]	Methodology [ ]	Results of Research [ ]	Analysis of Research [ ]
Conclusion [ ]	References [ ]	**HOORAY**	**IT IS**	**OVER!!!**

References

Allen, B. (1996). *Information tasks: Toward a user-centered approach to information systems*. San Diego, CA: Academic Press.

American Psychological Association [APA]. (2010). *Publication manual of the American Psychological Association*. Washington, DC: American Psychological Association.

Arias, K. (2007). "Even though it was the largest paper I ever wrote, it was made less difficult as we completed it section by section." Statement. Gill St. Bernard's School, Gladstone, New Jersey.

Barback, E. (2007). "The independent scientific research project at Gill St. Bernard's School prepared me for my experiences at Sarah Lawrence College." Statement. Gill St. Bernard's School, Gladstone, New Jersey.

Bates, M.J. (1989). *The design of browsing and berrypicking techniques for the online search interface*. Retrieved December 2, 2013 from University of California at Los Angeles, Graduate School of Library and Information Science Website: http://pages.gseis.ucla.edu/faculty/bates/berrypicking.html

Belkin, N.J. (1980). Anomalous states of knowledge as a basis for information retrieval. *Canadian Journal of Information Science, 5*, 133–143.

Bostian, L. (2007). "The benefits of this assignment go beyond the sciences." Statement. Gill St. Bernard's School, Gladstone, New Jersey.

Brown, C. (2013). "Sample reference list." Unpublished document. Gill St. Bernard's School, Gladstone, New Jersey.

Center for International Scholarship in School Libraries at Rutgers University [CISSL]. (2007). *Implementing guided inquiry through the school library*. Retrieved October 11, 2007 from http://www.cissl.scils.rutgers.edu/guided_inquiry/implementation.html

Council of Chief State School Officers (CCSSO) and National Governors Association (NGA). (n.d.). English Language Arts Standards » Home » English Language Arts Standards. *Common Core State Standards Initiative*. Retrieved November 30, 2013, from http://www.corestandards.org/ELA-Literacy

Donaldson, B. (2007). "Research changes the mind." Statement. Gill St. Bernard's School, Gladstone, New Jersey.

Duncan, T. (2007). "I found the analysis less difficult because I had guidelines to follow." Statement. Gill St. Bernard's School, Gladstone, New Jersey.

Edelman, H. (1998, January, 21). *Knowledge creation, production and distribution*. Lecture at Rutgers University, New Brunswick, New Jersey.

Eick, C., Meadows, L., & Balkcom, R. (2005, October). Breaking into inquiry: Scaffolding supports beginning efforts to implement inquiry in the classroom. *Science Teacher, 72*, 49–53.

EasyBib. http://content.easybib.com/students/guide-guide/mla/quick-guide/. Web

Gardner, H. (1993). *Frames of mind.* New York, NY: BasicBooks.

Geldzahler, H. (2013) "Comparisons of effects of dyslexia in six studies." Table. Gill St. Bernard's School, Gladstone, New Jersey.

Gunst, A. (2007). "I did my project on diabetes because of my mom." Statement. Gill St. Bernard's School, Gladstone, New Jersey.

Hesler, Claudia. (2010). *Database handout #1.* Unpublished document. Gill St. Bernard's School, Gladstone, New Jersey.

Hesler, C. (2013). "Easybib handout." Unpublished document. Gill St. Bernard's School, Gladstone, New Jersey.

Iannuzzi, P. (2000). *Information literacy competency standards for higher education.* Chicago, IL: Association of College and Research Libraries.

Illaria, S. (2013). "Learning how to do a proper research paper." Emory University, Atlanta, Georgia. Personal Communication.

Ireson, G. (2005). Einstein and the nature of thought experiments. *Journal School Science Review, 86,* 47–51.

Johnson, S. (2007). "The most important step in writing a scientific literature review." Statement. Gill St. Bernard's School, Gladstone, New Jersey.

Kuhlthau, C. (1991). Inside the search process: Information seeking from the user's perspective. *Journal of the American Society for Information Science, 42,* 361–371.

Kuhlthau, C. (1995). The instructional role of the library media specialist in the information-age school. In Carol Kuhlthau (Ed.), *Information for a new age: Redefining the library* (pp. 47–55). Washington, DC: American Library Association.

Kuhlthau, C. (2004). *Seeking meaning: A process approach to library and information services.* Westport, CT: Libraries Unlimited.

Kuhlthau, C. C., & Todd, R. J. (2007a). Constructivist learning and guided inquiry. *CISSL: Center for International Scholarship in School Libraries at Rutgers University.* Retrieved October 11, 2007, from http://cissl.scils.rutgers.edu/guided_inquiry/constructivist_learning.html

Kuhlthau, C. C., & Todd, R. J. (2007b). What is guided inquiry? *CISSL: Center for International Scholarship in School Libraries at Rutgers University.* Retrieved September 17, 2007, from http://cissl.scils.rutgers.edu/guided_inquiry/introduction.html

Kuhlthau, C. C., & Todd, R. J. (2007c). Implementing guided inquiry through the school library. *CISSL: Center for International Scholarship in School Libraries at Rutgers University.* Retrieved October, 2007, from http://cissl.scils.rutgers.edu/guided_inquiry/implementation.html.

Kuhlthau, C. C., & Todd, R. J. (2007d). Implementing guided inquiry at Gill St. Bernard's School, Gladstone, New Jersey. *CISSL: Center for International Scholarship in School Libraries at Rutgers University.* Retrieved December 6, 2007 from http://cissl.scils.rutgers.edu/guided_inquiry/casestudy.html.

Kuhlthau, C. C., Maniotes, L. K., & Caspari, A. K. (2007). *Guided inquiry: Learning in the 21st century.* Westport, CT: Libraries Unlimited.

Kuhlthau, C. C., Maniotes, L. K., & Caspari, A. K. (2012). *Guided inquiry design: A framework for inquiry in your school.* Santa Barbara: Libraries Unlimited.

Marsallo, M. (2007). "The guided inquiry program is a major reason why our students succeed." Statement. Gill St. Bernard's School, Gladstone, New Jersey.

Merhson, E. (2007). "This method made the process of writing my introduction uncomplicated." Statement. Gill St. Bernard's School, Gladstone, New Jersey.

Muench, J. (2007). Using a table, chart or graph. Unpublished document. Gill St. Bernard's School, Gladstone, New Jersey.

National Research Council [NRC]. (1996). *National science education standards.* Washington, DC: National Academy Press.

National Science Teachers Association [NSTA]. (2004). *National Science Teachers Association position statement: Scientific inquiry.* Retrieved December 2, 2013, from http://www.nsta.org/about/positions/inquiry.aspx

O'Connor, D. O. (1999). Class notes from a Needs Assessment lecture. Unpublished lecture at Rutgers University, New Brunswick, New Jersey.

Postlethwait, J.J., & Hopson, J. L. (2003). *Explore life.* Pacific Grove, CA: Brooks/Cole—Thomson Learning.

Puglisi, C. (2013). "The assignment timeline." Unpublished document. Gill St. Bernard's School, Gladstone, New Jersey.

Ripton, B. (1998). *Sophomore research paper assignment.* Unpublished document. Gill St. Bernard's School, Gladstone, New Jersey.

Rosenshine, B., & Meister, C. (1992). The use of scaffolds for teaching higher-level cognitive strategies. *Educational Leadership, 49,* 26–33.

Sherman, S. (2012). "Working as a researcher for a professor in the astronomy department." Penn State University, State College, Pennsylvania. Personal Communication.

Stil, M. (2007). "Here the student goes beyond the basic reporting of the peer reviewed studies." Statement. Gill St. Bernard's School, Gladstone, New Jersey.

Stil, M. (2007). "A student who learns how to write an abstract is learning how to write like a scientist." Statement. Gill St. Bernard's School, Gladstone, New Jersey.

Taeschler, J. (2007). "The cornerstone of science." Statement. Gill St. Bernard's School, Gladstone, New Jersey.

Wendell, M. (2007). "My friendly librarian suggested that I consider having the kids become their own experts." Statement. Gill St. Bernard's School, Gladstone, New Jersey.

Index

About the Authors

RANDELL K. SCHMIDT is the head librarian of Gill St. Bernard's School in Gladstone, NJ. Her published work includes Libraries Unlimited's *Lessons for a Scientific Literature Review: Guiding the Inquiry* and *A Guided Inquiry Approach to High School Research*. She holds a master of divinity degree from Princeton Theological Seminary and a master of library science degree from Rutgers University.

MAUREEN M. SMYTH is the school library media specialist at South Hunterdon Regional High School in Lambertville, NJ. Prior to that, she served as a librarian at Rutgers University, Princeton Public Library, and Gill St. Bernard's School. Smyth's past professional experience includes 17 years in the archaeology and museum fields. A graduate of Rutgers University with a bachelor degree in archeology and anthropology, she holds a master's degree in archeology from Boston University and a master of library and information science degree from Rutgers University.

VIRGINIA K. KOWALSKI, MLS, received her master's degree in library science from Rutgers University, New Brunswick, NJ. As a teaching librarian in both the middle school and upper school at Gill St. Bernard's School, she was instrumental in developing and implementing programs that involved the understanding of information literacy. Kowalski worked in the library and classroom independently and collaboratively to develop the writing/research program at Gill St. Bernard's.